*Living Legends*
*of the Santa Fe Country*

A pictorial guidebook for those looking for the strange and wonderful in "the land of enchantment."

Alice Bullock is Book Editor of the Santa Fe DAILY NEW MEXICAN, in which some of these stories and photographs have appeared.

# LIVING LEGENDS

## of the
## SANTA FE COUNTRY

## by *ALICE BULLOCK*

Revised and Enlarged

**the sunstone press**
Santa Fe, New Mexico / 1972

TO

Husband Dale who uncomplainingly subsidized Maryland Club, Marlboro and Chevron corporations while I worked

and

Fellow newshens Ann Clark, Holly Bond and Leslie Bottorff at the New Mexican.

Printed in the United States of America

Library of Congress Catalog Card Number 72-90383
International Standard Book Number 0-913270-06-7

First Edition (Green Mountain Press) 1970
Second Edition (Sunstone Press), Rev. and Enl. 1972

Printed by Starline, Albuquerque, New Mexico

# Contents

v

ILLUSTRATIONS:
In addition to photographs by the author, the following
illustrations are presented in this book:

## *Acknowledgments*

Thanks go to so many in the compiling of these legends. They are not originals, not creative writing, only a recalling, researching into the oral and written that has gone before.

For Elizabeth Willis De Huff, who listened to the same drum before the century had turned the halfway mark, there is a special niche in my personal Hall of Fame. Not only her own efforts as published in the now out of print "Say the Bells of Old Missions" but her charming and encouraging letters to the writer have been of inestimable help. The screen that stood before her Santa Fe fireplace now stands before mine. I try!

To Holly Bond, Pasatiempo Editor at the *New Mexican* a special pedestal with a legend of its own beginning "Encouragement and help." To Todd Webb who labored to teach me the mechanics of capturing sites with a camera "Thanks" seems inadequate.

Most of all, of course, to my husband Dale, otherwise familiarly known as Pappy. He suffered far more than I during the work. Coming home to a dark house with unwashed dishes, unmade beds and unthawed dinner because Ma was hunting legends at Chimayo, in the Salines, climbing Black Mesa, or sitting with knowledgeable tellers of tales wherever they would sit with me.

For all the State Library staff, particularly Virginia Jennings, I'll be back. There's at least one more river to cross, and you people provide great paddles cheerfully and efficiently.

ALICE BULLOCK

Santa Fe, New Mexico
February 1970

# Introduction

A collection of legends has nothing to do with the weighty academic studies of the historian or the purist. Legends cannot be proved, nor completely disproved. Sometimes they sound highly improbable, but for the over-30 reader, much in our daily news sounds the same way. A display of rocks from the moon can be seen, but deep in our inmost hearts that is harder to believe than the statue of San Jose not wanting to leave the little valley at Cienega or the healing qualities of the holy dirt at Santuario. These things are here; we grew up with them, while the moon was high above for lovers and lunatics.

Historical perspective is needed for enjoyment of the legends, and it is just possible that science, or documents newly discovered, will someday prove the history we accept today to be flawed. New Mexico highways now have historical markers lauding Espejo for his brave selfless explorations and yet it is known that he was actually running from the law in Mexico — a convicted murderer.

Our legends are not repeated here for the historian, but for enjoyment. They are of the folk, and among the ordinary people their own father, son, cousin or neighbor who goes to Vietnam is far closer than President Nixon or any other notable. For the New Mexican, Pearl Harbor is a historical footnote to what happened to our own 200th on Bataan. So with our legends and folklore.

Yet the generations gap operates here too. The old legends are being forgotten, and some of us do not want them to be. We love them. We want to share.

SANTUARIO
— India ink drawing by the late Thomas Wood Stevens

# I

*Village of Chimayo*

# Sacred Soil at Santuario

France has Lourdes. Canada has St. Anne's. New Mexico has El Santuario de Chimayo. To each of these sites pilgrims have carried their own mustard seed of faith and found miraculous healing for bodily ills.

El Santuario is an unpretentious little chapel in the village of Chimayo, 38 miles north of Santa Fe on State Highway 76. New Mexico is replete with lovely little chapels, but this one is different. It has a tiny candle-lit room at the left of the altar centered with a hole of sacred soil, the Mecca for palsied old ones, crippled children, veterans of Bataan and Vietnam, the weak and ailing.

On the walls of the anteroom are rows of crutches of those who have hobbled in to walk out cured.

The holy dirt from this hole in the ground has been carried away by the faithful for decades, yet the hole grows no larger — it is always miraculously replenished.

The chapel itself was believed completed in 1816. There are a number of legends concerning the site, having in common the appearance of an unearthly apparition. Some of these stories center on Bernardo Abeyta,

SACRED SOIL — As the visitor sees Santuario

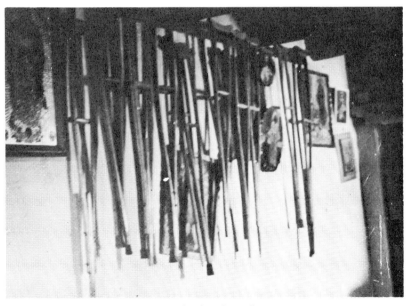

SANTUARIO — Crutches line the walls in anteroom

rich land owner of this region, being divinely cured when perilously near death.

One version tells that Abeyta, gravely ill, saw the image of his patron saint shimmering in the air across the acequia, and the saint beckoned him forward. Weakly he strove to obey; he fell exhausted on the ground where the vision had first appeared, and contact with the earth completely cured him.

Another legend has it that Dona Abeyta stood under the cottonwood trees bordering the acequia, praying for her husband who was so close to death that it was feared the priest from Santa Cruz would not be able to arrive in time. The vision came. It bade her take the dirt from this spot to her husband. Obeying, she saw Don Abeyta rise from his death bed completely cured.

Church records show that it was the Abeytas who built the chapel, and legend secures the site. Word of the miracle of Don Abeyta's healing was carried by word of mouth up and down the valley and over the mountains. The stream of pilgrims to the spot began, and continues. Today they arrive by car or truck, but frequently on foot in fulfillment of a vow, as often in thanks for prayers granted as for hopes of petitions for the present or future.

The faithful still kneel by the gaping hole, taking the soil with reverent hands, some mixing it with water and drinking it. Others rub the holy dirt on withered and shattered limbs or other diseased parts of the body for the cures they so confidently expect. Where the patient is too ill to make the journey, the dirt is carried to him.

In far villages mothers keep minute quantities on hand to use if a child becomes ill, or to toss a few grains into the fireplace to allay a storm and allow a husband or son to make his way safely home from a distant pasture or a long trip to a country store for supplies.

Other abuelos (old ones) will tell you that Don Abeyta was not ill at all; during Holy Week he was, as a good Penitente, performing his penance when he saw an unearthly glow coming from a hole in the ground near the Santa Cruz River. Rushing to the spot, with his bare hands he dug from the living earth the nearly six foot tall crucifix that now hangs back of the altar. He called his brother Penitentes, and a procession was formed to carry the crucifix to the church at Santa Cruz.

The next morning the crucifix was back in the hole where Abeyta had found it. Three times it was taken to Santa Cruz, and three times it reappeared in Chimayo in the original place. This was taken to be a command to build a chapel at the spot, and it was done.

Tied in with several of the minor legends of El Santuario are the two great cottonwoods that once raised great leafy arms in benediction immediately in front of the churchyard. One still stands, the other became a safety hazard and had to be removed.

One story has a foot protruding from a cottonwood trunk after the disappearance of a discouraged priest, who was unable to persuade the villagers to build a church here. Another story tells of a young girl finding the crucifix here when she went to the acequia for water. Regardless of which, if one accepts any version, the chapel houses beautiful examples of the work done by early day santeros (saint makers). The hand carved doors and corbels attest to the devotion and skill of the mountain-bred artisans.

Church records would seem to authenticate the Abeyta legend more than any of the other legends that have grown up around the chapel. The full story of El Santuario and other versions of the many legends concerning it are given in a booklet by Stephen F. de Borhegi, entitled "El Santuario de Chimayo." It was published by the Spanish Colonial Arts Society in 1956, and is still available.

Don Abeyta died in 1856, leaving a widow and eight children. By special permission from Bishop Lamy, he was buried in El Santuario, the chapel of Our Lord of Esquipulas.

El Santuario has been the subject of many controversies, and during the depression it was almost lost. As a private chapel, as it had been until this time, it was sold and the beautiful santos, bultos and paintings were auctioned off to private buyers. A group of people, interested in keeping El Santuario intact, bought back the precious furnishings, and turned the chapel to the church.

Today the faithful, the curious, the tourist, the devout and the unknowing visit El Santuario in a never-ending procession. When the sun

ORIGINAL CRUCIFIX and GATEWAY to Camposanto in front of Santuario

is warm, gentle Pablo Medina, the elderly sacristan, sits on the long wooden bench outside the church, greeting all impartially and benignly. Inside, in incense filled air, candles flicker, people look and leave, or kneel in prayer before the altar.

DESCANSO—Resting place enroute to Camposanto

# Santo Who Wears Out His Shoes

The mountain villages of New Mexico are always beautiful, but never more so than in December when these deeply religious communities are honoring the birth of Santo Nino, the Holy Child. In many the old folk plays are reenacted, while winding mountain roads and adobe homes are lighted with the flickering gleam of luminarios and farolitas. The deep, rich peal of church bells is caught by stark sandstone cliffs in the canyons, and echoes reverberate on a descending scale. "Unto us a child is born . . ."

Today roofs of small adobe homes more often than not reach for

WORN LITTLE SHOES of Santo Nino displayed in the church of Santo Nino de Atoche in Chimayo

air waves that bring New York, Hollywood, London with TV antennas, but it was not always thus. Niches in thick old walls still hold beloved saints, and legends are still told of the intervention of these saints in daily life. And why not? The church was the warp upon which was woven the woof of living. No santo was or is more beloved than Santo Nino.

Sometimes a lonely woman, her devout prayers unanswered, took the santo (saint) from his niche and banished Him to the depths of a storage chest. Such a story is told of Placitas by E. Boyd. A child was stolen by the Navajo, and the distraught mother calloused her knees before the Santo Nino, praying fruitlessly, for the return of her child. In her anguish she put Santo Nino out of sight. Her own sight was too often blurred with tears.

Then came the day when she heard the muffled sound of bells coming from the storage chest. Opening it she took Santo Nino from his place of banishment and put Him back in the vacant niche.

There came a fumbling with the latch on the door, and the long lost son burst into the room. The rounding up of the Navajo for the long walk to Bosque Redondo had given the child an opportunity to escape, and Santo Nino had guided him home.

Legends concerning the Santo Nino are not confined to Hispanic culture. The Indians have many and perhaps the most human is one of simple faith. It concerns an early day Indian pueblo, although which pueblo is a matter of choice, for this legend has been told of San Juan, Nambe, San Ildefonso, Isleta and Tesuque.

It seems that there had been a long drought, so severe that even the sturdy leaves of the corn plants hung limp on the stalk; bean plants were sere and lifeless, and the melon vines had curled under the relentless sun. Rain dances had been danced, but there was no rain.

Perhaps the new God of the Spaniard would help them! In a body they went to the padre at the mission church and asked him for permission to carry the Santo Nino around the fields. "Surely," they asserted. "He will help us when he sees the need."

The good padre nodded his head. He, too, was worried. Many would die during the coming winter if there were no food.

Solemnly they carried Santo Nino around the fields, across the dry arroya, up and down the canyon in the twilight of yet another rainless day before returning Him to the church.

It was midnight when they roused to hear that most welcome sound — rain. Lots of rain. Every little gulley ran with the sky. Now fear came. Had they prayed too long? The rain ran in torrents, and weakened roots were torn from the once hard earth. Corn stalks swirled in the muddy flood, raced down the canyon in sodden disarray. Morning sun revealed complete desolation.

Once again the Indians went to the church. Kneeling, they begged

7

SANTO NINO in his special case in Chimayo church

the priest, "Father, let us take the Holy Mother to the fields," they implored.

"Why?" he asked, sadly looking into their upturned faces.

"So that She can see what her bad little boy has done," they answered.

Common too is the legend that Santo Nino often leaves the church during the hours when animals, birds and people sleep. He goes on errands of mercy, soothing the feverish child, easing pain, listening to the prayers of a worried mother. No one sees Him, but the evidence is there for all to marvel at. His little shoes are scuffed and worn.

This belief remains strong in the village of Chimayo, some 38 miles north of Santa Fe. The story is told by parishioners of Santuario and also by those of the church dedicated to Santo Nino, which is scarcely a stone's throw from the much more widely known Santuario.

There is rivalry between the two churches, and where advocates vouch for the authenticity of the legend, each may discount it for the rival church. Both agree that there is a special blessing to be gained by supplying new baby shoes for the little santo.

In the Santo Nino church (privately owned but open to the public) a pair of tiny worn white shoes are on display, silently attesting to the veracity of their claim for their Santo Nino. Here too are names handwritten on slips of paper and pinned to the robes of the santos. Sometimes instead of a name, for whom special blessings are sought, there will be pinned the picture of a child, or the treasured likeness of a young man in uniform.

Flickering candles in ruby glass answer no questions, preach no sermons. They burn, while the odors of beeswax and incense mingle in the subdued light. A shawled woman genuflects and kneels to say her rosary. Legends or no legends, one thing is certain. Here is Faith — the faith of our fathers.

NAMBE FALLS — A girl of the pueblo in her
ceremonial finery waits beside the falls
— Photo by John V. Young

# III

## *Stolen Holy Water*

For the casual visitor, Nambe is the friendliest of all the pueblos. No tall terraced pueblo here, but a scattering of comfortable-looking farm homes, some looking old, others as though they were model homes of the latest real estate development around the larger towns. Only the kiva in the old plaza proclaims this to be the home of the old gods.

The setting is, however, far more beautiful than most. The soft roll of the hills, the weird rock formations, the misty mountain backdrop must be seen to be appreciated.

Back up on the mountain slope is Nambe Falls, and the legend here has an almost classical Greek simplicity. The upper falls is called Mountain Lad, the lower one is Arrow Dart. Their source, says an old story, is a beautiful maiden's tears. This maiden had two suitors for her hand, a warrior called Arrow Dart, and a hunter known as Mountain Lad. She favored Mountain Lad.

One morning she set out to take Mountain Lad some freshly baked tortillas, even though the day was a rainy one. They often met on the mountain slope.

When she arrived at their trysting place, the maiden found Mountain Lad dying from wounds inflicted by the jealous Arrow Dart. As she raised her face, wet with rain and tears, she saw Arrow Dart watching from the ravine just above her.

Raising her hands, she called on the Sun God, the Thunderbird and the Spirit of the Mountain to avenge Mountain Lad's death. Arrow Dart feared her curse, and raised his bow to slay her as well. The Gods had heard the maiden and as he sprang forward the earth opened, and he sank from sight, and with him the body of the slain hunter.

Desolately the girl wandered, weeping, and wherever she rested her tears formed small pools, springs that trickled down toward the ravine, and into the cleft that had swallowed up her lover and his murderer. Her tears continue to spill down the mountain side as the Nambe Falls. Once a year there are ceremonial dances here by the Nambe Indians, and visitors are welcome.

OLD HOUSE opposite the kiva at Nambe Pueblo

This all happened long before the Spaniard came, but the maiden's tears still rush downward, and all who see them marvel at their beauty.

When the first colonizer, Onate, settled not too far from Nambe at San Juan de los Caballeros, the Nambe Indians were very curious. Here were men who were not only warriors, but who rode miraculous beasts with big, ugly teeth. They had strange medicine men as well. This was understandable to the Indian. He, too, had different clans — the warrior people, the winter clan people, and the caciques who were the priests in pueblo life — the medicine men.

It was the business of the Indian medicine men to study and learn what was pleasing to the Gods who dwelt everywhere — in the sun, stars, wind, plants, trees, the very earth.

Gods were good and helped the Indian, but there were witches who made bad things happen. They must be guarded against. Medicine men had to have many charms, spells, rituals to ward off evil and gain favor with the good.

One Nambe medicine man looked at his feathers — eagle, owl, bluejay. They were potent. He looked at his bags of cornmeal, pollen and the sacred salt from the salt lakes behind the mountains to the south (Estancia Valley). They, too, were strong magic. But these white men had a magic also, the cross with the dead man, and the holy water.

The Indian could not really understand the crucifix, but the holy water was perhaps a new magic that he might use successfully if he could but learn the proper ritual and way of using it.

Nambe's medicine men went often to the kiva of the white medicine man, the kiva he called a church. Finally one of their medicine men came to Nambe. The people helped this padre build a big kiva for the new way, though it was not round as Indians ordinarily make their kivas. This certainly was different magic!

Our particular medicine man watched more closely than any of the other Indians. He secretly practised doing everything in the white man's ritual in exactly the same way. The sign of the cross in the air, the words (which meant nothing to him) he learned by rote. But where was he to get some of the holy water? Spells could not be worked without it.

One evening, when dark blanketed the white man's kiva this bronze-skinned medicine man went to the church and carried away with him a small olla of the holy water.

NAMBE — Kiva in plaza of the pueblo

At home he looked at it carefully, smelled it, shook it gently. Nothing happened. A finger poked tentatively into the olla merely felt wet. Holding it up he watched, analyzed minutely. The finger dried off as does the rain when the sun once again shows his face. Fearfully he raised the olla to his lips and tasted it. It was just like the water from the Falls, or from the river which now was low with little water running. The snow gods had left the mountains and would not be back until the moon of the yellow leaves.

He knew dance steps must be right or the good would not come. Perhaps the holy water was no good without the ritual. He called his wife.

"To your knees," he commanded and she obeyed. Just exactly as he had seen the padre do, he repeated the white man's movements, words and then generously sprinkled her with the water in the olla.

Instead of her usual compliance, she rebelled. "The white man's magic is not for us," she complained. "I feel nothing but wet, and I am afraid that witches will take me and our children!"

Fearfully they watched the balance of the night, seeking to read the omens of the clouds that passed before the moon, the call of the night birds, the bark of the coyote. When dawn came they went to the river.

With the sacred amole, yucca root, she bathed carefully and washed her beautiful long black hair thoroughly, while the river carried away the suds of the amole and the taint of the holy water. Every garment she had worn was just as carefully cleansed to rid it of any magic qualities stored in the holy water. When one does not know, it is well not to try to do another's spells!

The white man did not know Indian magic either, and much later a medicine man from Nambe was hanged as a witch by the Spanish. The priest at Nambe testified that he felt curious, sharp pains in his back when this Indian was near him, that he was often ill for no reason because the Indian had cast a spell on him.

The priest and the pagan were both honorable men.

Nambe is 21 miles north of Sante Fe, and is a lovely place to visit. When dances are held, they are exceptionally well performed.

# A Bell for Don Angelo

Rich as this region is in legends, none surpass the lovely ones centered in the ancient village church at Santa Cruz. Here in the shadow of the towering Sangre de Cristo (Blood of Christ) mountains are two old legends and one that is comparatively recent.

Santa Cruz de la Canada, just out of Espanola, was once a bigger city than Santa Fe. We are not sure of the founding date, but records show that Luis Quintana was alcalde mayor at the time of the Pueblo Rebellion of 1680.

Legend says that during this very early period there came to Santa Cruz a very young man, Don Angelo, from far away Spain. Like so many of his countrymen in the early 1600's, he had heard the tales of infinite riches in this new land across the seas, and was fired with the ambition to gain some of this wealth for himself.

Don Angelo had a very strong motive to spur him on. He had just become betrothed to the fairest senorita in the Castilian village in which he lived — if indeed not all of Spain. He would go to the new world and bring back the wherewithal to buy everything for his Teresa.

Before he sailed for America he gave his love a golden ring and a delicate gold chain and cross.

Alas, after the perilous journey Don Angelo found less gold in this new country than was molded into his parting gift to Teresa. His heart must have been very heavy as he walked the rutted dirt roads of this mountain village called Santa Cruz. Perhaps thoughts of his far away love were in his mind when the savage yells came. The village was being raided by the Apache!

Indian raids were not unusual in the mountain villages. They had been a part of the life of the Pueblo Indians from the beginning, and continued after the arrival of the Spaniard. The raiders were the roving bands — Apache, Ute and sometimes Navajo.

When the raid was over Don Angelo lay dead. He would never return to Castile and Teresa.

At long last the news of his fate reached Spain. Teresa was heartbroken, and the villagers there shared in her grief. It was decided to cast a bell for the church in Santa Cruz in memory of Don Angelo.

THE CHURCH of the Holy Cross, Santa Cruz

As the molten metal for the bell bubbled, Teresa emerged from the home she had refused to leave even for mass after the tragic news had come. Slowly she walked to the simmering vat, and with streaming eyes dropped the ring, chain and cross into the cauldron.

The villagers, seeing what she had done, silently followed suit. Gold and silver buttons, earrings, precious pins, bracelets followed the ring and cross. Precious metals in a bell mellow and sweeten the tone.

If there be a faint echo of the pealing of the church bell at Santa Cruz when one is near the Church of the Holy Cross, villagers smile. It must be, they say, the anniversary of the death of Don Angelo.

As time went on, events crowded into and out of the little village of Santa Cruz. The reign of the King of Spain in Mexico ended, and this territory automatically became a part of Mexico. So far away, people here paid little attention until the Mexican government passed a tax bill in 1837.

There was strong opposition to the directly paid taxes in this northern province. Leaders of the opposition worked and talked to the villagers telling them that these taxes would have to be paid on all sorts of things. They enumerated such things as poultry and that "husbands would be taxed for the privileges generally attaching to connubial bliss."

In secret the people began to foment a rebellion. In this they had the sympathy and assistance of the Pueblo Indians in the northern part of the state, the whole centering in Santa Cruz. There had been

16

SANTO showing hand with missing fingers

hatred of the Spaniard in the Pueblos, but now these people had hope — for had it not been prophesied that a new race would come from the east to redeem them from the Spanish yoke soon?

The end result was a pitched battle at La Canada de Santa Cruz, and the rout of the insurrectionists. The Mexican government, in turn, yielded to the Army under General Kearney, and Santa Cruz became a part of the American territory along with the rest of New Mexico.

It was under the flag of the United States that another legend was born. Beautiful Santa Cruz became, as it is for many today, a haven of peace and quiet. Offering this, retired people of wealth began to come to this valley and buy homes.

One such elderly couple was completely charmed with their new home and the people living there. Seeing the condition of the ancient statue of Our Lady of Carmel in the church, they decided to do something for the village and the church.

Quietly, saying nothing to the Padre or villagers, they purchased a lovely new statue, all bright unchipped plaster and lovely fresh colors. When it arrived they went to the open church, took the time-eroded wooden statue from its niche and replaced it with the new one.

Morning came, and the couple heard chanting and singing coming up the long road to their house. Surely it was the villagers coming to

BELL TOWER and ancient bell of the
legend of Don Angelo

LA MADRECITA, the well beloved,
in the church at Santa Cruz

thank them for their gift, they thought, and went out on the portal to receive them.

The village alcalde stepped forth, leading a lovely young maiden wearing her communion dress and veil.

"Your wife," the alcalde addressed the man, "is no longer pretty. She is wrinkled and old. You do not want her any longer. We have brought you a new wife, a young and pretty one. Here she is!"

Slowly the couple comprehended what was being told them by the villagers. The wife turned and walked into the house and returned with the old statue of Our Lady of Carmel. They now understood why the villagers called it La Madrecita — the Little Mother. La Madrecita was old, worn and unlovely to the casual eye — but she was loved. The new statue could not replace her.

Without a word the wife reverently placed the ancient statue in the arms of the maiden. The procession wheeled slowly and the hymns of praise and joy were carried skyward by the wings of their love. La Madrecita was returning home to her niche in the Church of the Holy Cross.

A third legend is tied to the missing fingers on another old Santo in the church. Two fingers are missing.

Arroyas in New Mexico, often dry, sometimes run dangerously high, threatening homes and lives. It is said that such was the case, long ago, when the river in Santa Cruz overflowed its banks, and continued to rise. Half of the village was in peril as torrents of rain continued to feed the flood. Finally desperate, a devout man broke off a finger of the statue and flung it into the flood with a prayer. The finger sank. The flood subsided and a wavering shaft of sunshine glistened on the decreasing muddy water of the stream.

The second missing finger stopped an epidemic of smallpox. Sometimes, before vaccination became a general practice, this dread disease walked the land and left a trail of death. The white towel on the gate marked many village homes, and everyone walked in fear. Even going to church on Ash Wednesday was fraught with fear and sorrow.

The second finger of the statue, says the legend, was burned and the ash used for marking the foreheads of the devout. Even the sight of the smudge was enough to kill the fatal germ — and the epidemic was over. Not another case was reported. The mutilated hand of the Santo remains to testify mutely to the efficacy of the holy faith.

# V

## *Indian Cinderella*

The Cinderella story has always been dear to the hearts of people everywhere whatever the guise it takes. There is a lovely Cinderella legend in one of the Pueblos north of Santa Fe, San Juan de los Caballeros (St. John of the Gentlemen on Horseback).

The events in this legend happened a little before once-upon-a time at San Juan. There were two sisters, the youngest one a beautiful girl, and a very dutiful daughter. Her sister wasn't really ugly, but she wasn't pretty either. The mother had been dead since before the younger daughter had first begun to walk, and the elder girl had to do all the household tasks and take care of her little sister.

When the younger girl became old enough to bring water from the spring, grind corn, tan hides and cook, the elder sister made her do all the work, while she sat and wove beautiful mantas for herself.

Not even the beautiful mantas brought her a husband, nor had all the time she spent washing her hair with yucca root brought a suitor. Those young men who came by their rooms in the pueblo always looked at the younger girl until the elder sister sent her on an errand or back inside the pueblo to rake up ashes. Then the young men went away.

One day there was great excitement in the pueblo. A runner had come from Abechiu Pueblo to invite the San Juan Indians to a great feast and fair at their pueblo. Always at these events there were competitions. For the women it was not only a chance to wear their most becoming mantas, but to show their skill at grinding corn, and perhaps be invited to dance.

Elder sister was particularly excited and happy. She had just finished a white manta with woven rainclouds and zig-zag lightning in black and red. It was the finest she had ever made. When she ground her corn, surely a young man would sit at the foot of her metate (grinding stone) and sing. She wouldn't mind living at Abechiu.

Young sister swept up the ashes with her willow broom and wept. She had nothing except her ragged manta. There had been no time to weave after all the household chores. When the appointed day arrived, she was the only maiden in the pueblo who did not pile her basket high with blue and white corn and go swinging along the trail to the four-day feast. Instead she sorrowfully took the big olla and walked toward the spring. At least she could wash her hair!

Then by the path she heard a man's voice. "You shall grind the finest corn at the Abechiu fair," the voice said. "Take the corn from this stalk." There was no one near but there by the path was a stalk of corn — and wonderful to behold — the corn was not blue and white as was all the corn then, but yellow and red. Surely the maiden thought, she would win with such beautiful corn.

But alas! Her manta was old and torn. No one would look at her with such a disreputable garment. Her eyes filled with tears. "Take the corn!" came the command again.

She blinked the tears away and as her eyes cleared she saw that she wore a manta more beautiful than anything she had ever seen. Her bare feet were covered with fawn skin moccasins as light as a dandelion seed, and stitched with such tiny stitches that they might have been made by Spider Woman herself.

Young sister eagerly filled the basket that was suddenly there, and danced away on the trail.

For three days at the fair her mano fairly flew over the metate,

COLORED CORN is honored in the basket dance of the San Juan Indians
— Photos by Tom McKinnon

and many there were who stopped to sing before her grinding stone. But she would dance with none of them. Their voices were not the voice she had heard by the path.

Many asked about the lovely young stranger who ground red and yellow corn, for none knew her in her splendid garb and her face was always down. On the fourth day, as she ground the last of her corn she heard a new voice, singing softly as the wind rustles in the corn leaves. It approached and stopped at her grinding stone. It was the voice of the Corn Boy! For the first time she raised her face, and held out her hand. With him she would dance. His clothing was as rich as her own.

When the drums at last were silent, younger sister lifted her basket of finely ground meal and slowly held it out to the stranger. Gravely he accepted, and carried it to the girl's father for his blessing.

Arrangements were made quickly for the wedding feast, and the basket dance was danced. Elder sister, with the beautiful younger one married, soon found herself a mate as well.

Today at San Juan, the basket dance is performed as the people celebrate again and again the gifts of the nature gods, and the special gift of the colored corn in that long ago time.

San Juan Indians, who helped the first colonists in New Mexico through their trying months of beginning, can claim that the first red and yellow corn was brought to them by a pretty Tewa Indian Cinderella.

DANCERS at a San Juan Pueblo festival

— Photos by Tom McKinnon

SAN JUAN Pueblo ceremonial dancers ready for their rare basket dance

ABIQUIU — Fallen cross at a Penitente morada

RUINS of the Santa Rosa de Abiquiu Mission

# *Curse of The Hidalgo*

To understand the legend of Santa Rosa de Abiquiu it is necessary to warm your hands at the fire of the past. North of Santa Fe on U.S. 84, is the Abiquiu that is now so peaceful, quiet and beautiful but it has not always been peaceful and quiet.

Tewa Indians once inhabited the valley. There was a pueblo at a place called La Puenta, a mesa on the south bank of the Rio Chama about three miles southeast of the present town of Abiquiu. It was called Abechiu, "hooting of an owl." This pueblo was abandoned, probably in the 1500's. Subsequently the valley and surrounding area became the home grounds of the Utes, Jicarilla Apaches and, in the extreme northwestern part, of the Navajo.

It was visited fairly often by the Comanches, sometimes by warriors in their campaigns against the Utes. Indians, prior to the coming of the Spaniards (and after!) were not all one big, happy family.

A Spanish town, called Abiquiu, was founded prior to 1747, for records exist showing that it was abandoned in August of that year after an attack by the Utes. It was resettled in 1754, but attacks were so frequent it was again abandoned. Mexican Governor Mendinueta compelled the settlers to reoccupy the site in 1770.

Our legend concerns a certain very rich Hidalgo during this period of unrest. He had a huge, hidebound chest into which he poured an ever growing horde of gold and silver coins while he dreamed of taking his wealth and retiring to Mexico City or perhaps even to Spain. So great was his desire for gold that he was stingy even with his only son. He did, however reluctantly, give to the padre of the little mission church of Santa Rosa de Abiquiu.

Came the day once again when the word was that the valley was being raided — this time by the Navajo. Most of the time Navajos raided for food, clothing and slaves to do the menial work that had to be done even in the most primitive tribes — gathering wood for cooking and warmth, moving camp, tanning hides, carrying water, cooking, gathering pinon nuts and other edibles. The Navajos had begun to learn the value of the gold and silver coins so prized by the Spaniards, and the rich Hidalgo knew this.

PENITENTE morada at Abiquiu

He quickly called a trusted servant, an Indian called Ramon. Unlocking the windowless room where the chest was stored, they dragged the heavy treasure out and loaded it on a two-wheeled cart, and whipped the horses into a run to reach the mission church.

The shouts of the Hidalgo brought the good padre out of the church as they clattered up.

"Padre! The Navajos are coming! Help us carry the chest into the church!"

The hesitant padre helped Ramon and the Hidalgo to carry the treasure into the church, the iron key which the Spaniard carried on his person day and night clanking as they struggled with the burden.

Quickly the three men, spurred by the frenzy of the Hidalgo, dug a hole in the dirt floor directly under the altar and placed the chest in it, and even more quickly filled it again.

"Place a curse upon anyone who disturbs this chest, Padre," the Hidalgo commanded, sweat trickling down his brow and into his well cared for beard.

"Placing a curse is a sin," the good padre demurred. Then he remembered that the old gentleman had always been relatively generous with the church, and he added, "We can ask a blessing though."

Raising his hands, he asked that the treasure bless only the Hidalgo and his son, the rightful owners.

"And be a curse to any other!" the frightened, but still insistent Hidalgo finished. Even as he spoke wild whoops were heard outside, and the door burst open as the Navajo surged into the church.

Ramon had gone to recapture the frightened horses that had, untended, run away. The padre and the Hidalgo were slain on the spot, their blood soaking down into the so recently disturbed earthen floor. The Indians took whatever appealed to them, and set fire to the woodwork and the altar of the church.

Many died that day, including the Hidalgo's son. The remaining villagers were hard put to survive and turned to the business of sustaining life and caring for the wounded.

Meanwhile, bandits had learned of the Hidalgo's wealth, his death, and the escape of the servant Ramon. Late one night they took Ramon prisoner and tortured him until he told where the chest was buried. Gathering picks and spades they forced Ramon to accompany them to the church ruin. The bandido chief was the first to sink a spade into the fire blackened earth. Before he could lift the first shovel of dirt he gave a strangled cry and fell to the ground dead.

Quaking in terror, the remaining bandits pulled their leader from the ruin, tied him on his horse, and sped over the moonless road, not looking back, never to return.

Bruised and battered Ramon told his friends what had happened. None wanted to brave the curse to try to recover the Hidalgo's treasure.

In more modern times, it is said, a couple of young men, not believing in the efficacy of any curse, dug for a short time at the ruin; finding nothing, they clambered into their pickup and drove away. The truck is supposed to have overturned before they got back to Espanola. Both were killed. "Excessive speed," read the police report, but there are those who whisper that it was the curse.

Today the site at Santa Rosa is posted as an antiquarian reserve and it is illegal to dig, pick up pottery sherds, or in any way to disturb the ruins of Santa Rosa. One wall remains and the door in it looks blankly out across the Rio Chama to the red and white bands of the mesas that climb to where the sun walks the sky.

No more do Indians raid. The Utes were moved to a reservation in Colorado, and their chief, Chico Belasquez, with his fantastic leggings is gone too. Those leggings were decorated with the entire fingernails of Americanos on one leg and Mexicanos on the other. Abiquiu was his favorite spot for collecting fingernails!

Abiquiu, a deeply religious community, was not long without a church after the burning of Santa Rosa. A new church was built in the center of the village, and today Hispano, Indian and Anglo children play in St. Thomas churchyard, supervised by Sister Anne. In addition two moradas, still in use, were constructed by that much maligned remnant of the Third Order of St. Francis, called the Penitentes.

The home of internationally famous artist Georgia O'Keefe, built high on a rock promontory, looks out over the winding river, the ancient cottonwoods in man-made groups, and the deserted lonely wall that once was part of the mission church of Santa Rosa.

BELL TOWER on a penitente
morada at Abiquiu

# *Taos — The Sacred Valley*

Taos (rhymes with 'house') is sometimes said to contain the oldest continuously occupied apartment houses in America. The Taos of modern times is really two villages, the Spanish village Don Fernando de Taos and the Pueblo of Taos. It is, despite the rich history of the village, the Pueblo that draws visitors from all over the world. The natural beauty of the entire valley, the Sacred Valley, presided over by brooding Taos Mountain, is no deterrent however!

There are two dominant legends besides the emergence myth about the founding of the Pueblo. The first legend says that the people were wandering in search of a home site. The caciques had told them they would know when they had found the place the Gods favored; they would find an eagle feather at the side of a stream. When they wearily trudged into Taos Valley, there was the stream laughing its way over stones and through lush grasses, bordered by thickets of plum bushes. There, too, was the eagle feather — but across the stream was still another feather — hence pueblos were built on both sides.

A friendly rivalry between the two pueblos grew up, with the selection of the ruling chief for both pueblos being ascertained by races, climbing of the pole, and other contests as decreed by the Gods through the medicine men. Today the outward sign of governorship is in the cane given the pueblo by Abraham Lincoln while he was president. These canes (given to all the major pueblos) have become precious relics wherever they are, and pass from one governor to the next as a mark of office.

The second and lesser known legend of the founding of Taos also accounts for the wearing of separated legs of trousers by Taos Indian men. The men wear plain or plaid cotton blankets — sometimes over their heads and falling in graceful lines to their knees; at other times the blanket is wrapped around the hips, with the ends tucked in as a turban is wrapped and secured.

In the second legend, the Taos Indians climbed a rainbow that dipped down sharply, ending in Taos Valley. Climbing it was slow, hard work, but once the apex had been reached, descending was so fast it wore out the seat of their pants! The male traditionalist at Taos today always

TAOS PUEBLO
— Photo by New Mexico State Tourist Bureau

wears his blanket in one approved way or another, though many of the young ones wear ordinary clothing at work, at school, and in Taos village.

Taos Pueblo, with its four and five storied terraced apartments was first visited by Europeans in August of 1541. Capt. Hernandez de Alvarado and a small detachment of soldiers from Coronado's expedition journeyed north up the Rio Grande to visit this large (now the largest) Indian pueblo. There are ruins of some ninety pueblos scattered through Taos Valley, indicating early populations, but just how large the present Pueblo was then is a bit uncertain. Early Spanish figures consistently tend to be a bit exaggerated.

Just as consistently, as Spaniards continued to make group forays into the northern outpost of Mexico that we now call New Mexico, each dubbed the pueblos with a different name or version of the Indian name. Taos, however, seems to run pretty consistently with the name it now bears, though the origin is uncertain.

Some there are who favor the theory that, coming from North China or Manchuria in their intercontinental migration, they brought with them a lingering memory of Laotze and his doctrine of Taoism. Others believe the Spaniard gave them the name Taos because the warriors carried shields marked with a red cross like the Greek letter Tau. Or could it have been based in the Taos Indian language? Their word for "Thank you" is "tao" and certainly the Spanish had much to thank these Indians for.

In 1598, 22 years before the Pilgrims landed at Plymouth Rock, a Spanish missionary, Padre de Zamora, was in residence at the pueblo, teaching the Indians the tenets of the Christian religion. Friar Pedro de Miranda went to Taos in 1613 and found a church (the mission of San Geronimo) already under construction.

The village of Taos, a walled town, was built around the present plaza in 1615. The Spaniard, with his superior armaments, could be of real help in repelling nomadic Comanche invaders that were a constant menace, particularly at harvest time.

In 1680, when the great Indian rebellion came, Taos Indians not only joined whole heartedly in killing or driving out the Spaniard, they were ringleaders. De Vargas and his men reconquered New Mexico in 1692, but Taos continued to hold out another four years.

De Vargas and his troops went north in September of 1696 to claim the allegiance of Taos for the King of Spain. The Indians fled to the mountains, and it was the heavy snows there that forced them down into the valley and the waiting De Vargas.

Friendly relations being restored, the partially-ruined church was rebuilt, and during the next century the Spaniards built their haciendas up and down the valley. With vassals and Indian slaves they dug acequias (irrigation ditches) and crops were abundant. Flocks of sheep were grazed on the mountain slopes, and the population was almost self sustaining.

With wool for weaving, hides of deer, elk and antelope to tan for leather, and plenty of food they had a surplus for trade. The caravans from Chihuahua bringing sugar, coffee, silks and linens for sale and trade were eagerly welcomed, and Taos became a trade center for the entire area, eventually extending as far as the Missouri.

French trappers and plains Indians learned of the Taos Fairs

A TAOS BOY has a head start on his dog as he
hurries to a Head Start class

TAOS WOMEN still chop holes in the Rio to dip
water for household use

and the trade fair became an annual affair not to be missed. In 1805 the first Anglos — trappers and traders — were delighted to find such a haven as Taos provided, and it became very popular with the mountain men. Kit Carson (his home is a visitor's must in the village now) was one of these.

Carson eventually made Taos his home. Albert Pike, Dick Wootton, Gov. Charles Bent, Padre Jose Antonio Martinez, Ceran St. Vrain, Judge Beaubien, other illustrious names from our history books knew Taos or made it their home base.

Padre Martinez — thought by many to be one of the most intelligent men of this period, not only ministered to the spiritual needs of the people, but published *El Crepusculo* the first newspaper west of the Mississippi in 1835. He organized the first school in the area, and was a civic and political leader as well. When Bishop Lamy came to Santa Fe, Padre Martinez did not always see eye to eye with this new French dignitary and eventually was excommunicated — in 1856. Mementos of this colorful Padre are on display in the Kit Carson Museum in Taos. He continued with his school and church until his death.

Charles Bent, one of the founders of Bent's Fort in Colorado was murdered in his home in Taos during the defiance of Mexican occupation forces, and his home, too, is a visitor's must. It was at this time (1847) that the old church at Taos Pueblo was destroyed by shells of Col. Price's cannon when the conspirators took refuge there.

One of the very few places where the United States flag may be flown day AND night is in Taos plaza. In 1861 there were numerous Confederate sympathizers in Taos, and several times these people had hauled down the Union standard and hoisted the Confederate flag. Capt. Smith Simpson, Kit Carson, Col. St. Vrain and Lt. Todd nailed the stars and strips to a tall cottonwood pole, erected it in the plaza, then retired to St. Vrain's store on the south side of the plaza, from which point they stood guard. The flag has waved there, day and night, since that time.

In 1889 two artists, Bert Phillips and Ernest Blumenschien, came over Taos Pass in a wagon. The rugged terrain resulted in a broken wagon wheel, and by the time it was repaired they were so enamoured with the beauty of the region and the Taos Indians that they never went on. They were the founders of the now internationally famous artists colony, for other artists, seeing their canvases, soon joined them and many stayed to win their own fame here in the shadow of the Sacred Mountain. They still come, for the beauty is still there. Whole books not only can be but have been written about Taos and the story is not yet complete.

Paved roads now make the trip to Taos an easy and pleasant one, but wild iris still color the pastures with the blue of the sky, and clouds

BACKYARD at the Taos Pueblo

TAOS PUEBLO — where walls were breached during the rebellion

of plum blossom drift along the fences in the spring. When autumn comes, aspen, evergreen and low-growing scrub oak vie in greens, golds and deep reds for a beauty that not even the best of artists can capture.

Fiestas, Indian dances, processions preserve the fine traditions that supplement the visual delight that is the "Sacred Valley" — Taos Valley.

EARLY DAY truck and limousine. A survivor of colonial times
in Taos. Now in the patio at the Kit Carson Museum

RUINS of old San Geronimo
Mission at Taos

35

MISSION CHURCH at Ranchos de Taos seen from the back — a favorite view of artists

# VIII

*Village of Ranchos de Taos*

## Ranchos de Taos Mystery

A metal pole at the side of Highway 64 four miles south of Taos holds a black lettered white sign saying simply "Ranchos de Taos." Such an unimaginative sign might announce Podunk, Indiana or Coffeyville, Kansas — but there would not follow the delight of seeing the quaint little adobe village that is Ranchos.

Speed limit signs are equally prosaic but only a barbarian or a resident needs them. The paved highway (the only paving in the village) passes the back side of the ancient mission church dedicated to St. Francis of Assisi.

There may well be an artist or so seated on a canvas camp chair busily trying to capture on canvas the majesty and beauty of those massive, buttressed walls of the church.

This church has stood solidly, a refuge for residents during roving Indian raids over 200 years ago, a refuge for the weary spirit from the hurly-burly world of today.

The camposanto — cemetery — in front of the church is walled in with a low wall, but a cross-surmounted wide portal gateway leads in to the huge, hand carved wooden doors. They are open from 6 a.m. to 6 p.m. every day, and in summer months there is a nightly lecture at 9 p.m. Then one may see, and experience, the "mystery" painting at the right of the altar.

The painting is called "Shadow of the Cross." In daylight or artificial light it depicts Jesus standing on the shore of the Sea of Galilee. We are all familiar with the phenomena of eyes, in a painting, seeming to be looking directly at us, regardless of which angle we stand in relation to the canvas. In this painting the whole body, not merely the eyes, seems to face the viewer, regardless of where he may be standing. There is another phenomenon, however, that is far stranger.

When lights are turned off and complete darkness prevails, the painting becomes another one completely. The background takes on a luminous glow, not unlike moonlight. The shadowed figure of Jesus changes posture, a cross appears over the left shoulder and a halo appears above his head. Snap the light back on, and once again there is the quiet figure by the sea.

This painting was executed two years before the discovery of radium by a Canadian artist, Henri Ault. It was a mystery to him, too. He disclaimed any knowledge of the reason for the change, saying

RANCHOS DE TAOS mission church

37

SHADOW OF THE CROSS as seen in
darkness. It required an exposure of
one hour to secure this print.
— Photo by Verne Sackett

that he believed himself demented when he went into his studio at night and discovered the luminosity. He called in friends — and they, too, could see what happened to this art work.

No explanation has yet been found. Sir William Crookes, a British physicist, was the first to try to discover the reason — unsuccessfully. No luminous paint has yet been developed that will not oxidize and darken within a relatively short time. More recent tests with Geiger counters, light tests and scrapings have revealed nothing as to the reasons for the change when exposed to light and darkness.

The Shadow of the Cross painting was exhibited in galleries in all parts of Europe and North America before being purchased in 1948 from an Atlanta, Georgia gallery by Mrs. Herbert Sydney Griffin of Wichita Falls, Texas and Ranchos de Taos for the Ranchos mission church.

A second piece of art work that carries its own mystery is now on display in this lovely mission church. In 1966 the condition of the church had become so deplorable that a complete renovation became imperative, bringing on a community controversy. The roof was leaking badly, the old vigas were seriously decomposed at the point where they rested on the aged adobe walls.

Plastering of the 4 to 6 foot thick walls, which had in modern times taken several hundred parishioners nine days to complete, was no longer adequate. Artists and lovers of the old arts were afraid that a renovation would spoil this beautiful church. But something had to be done!

Under the leadership of a dynamic priest, Father Manuel Alvarez, the church is now "more original than ever." John Gianardi, who specializes in the restoration of old buildings was commissioned for the task. So delicate was the work that loyal parishioners could be of little help, but at a cost of $74,000 the restoration was accomplished.

Inside and out, the work was thorough. In tearing out the confessional walls, a workman discovered a framed bas relief of St. Anthony. Why was it there? No one knows. How long had it been there? No one knows that either, but on the back are some almost illegible initials and the word "Quito."

Father Alvarez, originally from Quenca, Ecuador, is morally certain this art work came from his native country because of the frame. It is decorated with bits of mirror glass in a manner and style not practised anywhere else other than in Ecuador. St. Anthony is now with the other decorations used in the church.

Beautiful old art work, paintings, statuary and other objects in the church have been valued at a half million dollars or more, though this value would not be possible on the open market without substantiating church records. It takes the proof of their antiquity to establish their monetary value.

Most of the old vigas have been replaced, but the hand carved, vegetable dye painted corbels are original. The distinctive Santos of the 17th century are still here, and the old silver processional crucifix and chimes are still in constant use.

There is now a floor (under which repose the bones of many early parishioners) and today there are Spanish colonial type pews blending gracefully with the restored splendor of early days. Originally the mission floors were hard packed earth, and worshippers stood or knelt during services. Electric lights supplement the candlepower of days gone by, but their light is purposely diffused, soft.

Father Alvarez recalls when, during the first year of his tenure at Ranchos, he was told bluntly, "The church must be extensively repaired or it will be condemned." The Ranchos community is not a wealthy one. It seemed hopeless, but he remembered the words spoken to Francis of Assisi in a 13th Century vision, "Go, Francis, repair My church for it is nearly falling down."

Father Alvarez believed the St. Francis of Assisi Mission could be repaired, restored. It was a proud and happy priest who participated in the re-dedication services in the summer of 1967. With him, in addition to the parishioners participating in the ceremony, were Archbishop Davis and 60 priests of the diocese.

There is no fee for the summer evening lectures, but donations are gratefully received.

THE "MAGIC" PAINTING as seen
in daylight or artificial light.
— Photo by Verne Sackett

EAGLE DANCERS at San Ildefonso Pueblo
— Photo by New Mexico State Tourist Bureau

IX        *San Ildefonso Pueblo and Black Mesa*

# *The Dancers Who Never Returned*

In Indian country, a polite person does not ask an Indian his name. Instead he will ask the man before him or after him the name of his friend. On a limited basis at least this holds true in gathering legend or folklore. Gentle, kindly people will tell the seeker bits of folklore, but always it didn't happen at this pueblo, but at another one close by.

Most of the pueblos have a legendary giant, under whatever name given him in their particular version. Do not Anglos have Jack the Giant Killer? At San Ildefonso the legendary giant Tsah-ve-voh (Tsaviyo, Tsave Yoh) lived on Black Mesa. In some versions of the legend, Tsaviyo still comes down from this great, flat topped volcanic extrusion once a year when he whips men, women and children if they have

CEREMONIAL CIRCLE on top of Black Mesa,
to valley beyond and far below.

not been good during the year. In days before the days of old he even ate naughty children. He is still used as a threat to the misbehaving young — "The giant will whip you if you do that!"

Older children are not deterred. They know that the Twin War Gods, the Hero Twins, killed the giant and his family long ago so that the Pueblo people could travel to the springs safely, but he still lives in ceremonial ritual.

Black Mesa is rich in legend and history — some lost, some known, some yet waiting the archaeologists' patient toil. Before the Tewatowa peoples (San Ildefonso, San Juan, Santa Clara, Nambe and Tesuque) settled in the great river valley, other people lived on Black Mesa. Remains of their pit houses are distinguishable as much too regular ridges and depressions, now blanketed with low-growing grama grass and occasional patches of prickly wild creeping phlox.

Permission to climb Black Mesa is readily given by the San Ildefonso governor, Abel Sanchez, or his completely charming and lovely secretary. The Pueblo is 22 miles from Santa Fe, just off U.S. 84 on N.M. 4.

The Governor's office is opposite the church and is as modern as a national bank in appointments. A plaque on the wall behind his turquoise blue telephone attests that his phone is the two millionth to be installed by the telephone company. This office is as friendly and attentive as a long ago country store. A photography fee, collected here, goes to augment a scholarship fund.

Following the path worn by centuries of bare and moccasined feet up the steep talus slope on one side of the mesa is not easy. Frequent puffing pauses are necessary for most people as the faint trail climbs higher and higher toward the narrow notch in the basalt cliffs, and then you are on top. From here you can see forever. Villages and farms, the Otowi Bridge over the Rio Grande and the water tower at Los Alamos, spread out as though seen from an airplane suspended in time. A meadowlark whistles, a rabbit zig-zags, and from far below the engines of trucks on the highway preternaturally hum in a never ending stream of sound.

Under foot there is mystery. The stones on this volcanic mesa are not lava, but the river bottom variety, water rounded types that simply do not belong on a mountain top. How did they get here? There are thousands upon thousands of them.

We (Ruth McPherson accompanied me on the climb) searched for present day sacred fire shrines we had heard of. No sign of fire was found anywhere on the mesa top. One circle of volcanic rock centered with a white boulder was found on the side of the mesa facing the road leading to Puye. The boulder has two deep man-made indentations and two lesser ones, the sacred "four" of the Tewa world. Could this be an earth navel of the Tewa? We could only surmise and wonder, and sincerely hope that camera lenses were not profaning in any way. If they were, it was ignorance, not desire.

It was here on this mesa that the people of Tesuque, Nambe, San Ildefonso, Santa Clara, Pojoaque and Cuyamunge sought refuge when the Spanish soldiers raided their homes after the reconquest seeking food and slaves. Over a hundred Spanish soldiers stormed up the talus slope, only to be repulsed by arrows and rocks as they neared the notch at the top.

BLACK MESA seen from the back side, showing talus slide and trail site

43

The Spaniards won only when they had starved the Indians into surrender. During the long siege it is said that the Indian women sacrified their silky, long black hair to make a rope to hoist food and water over the cliffs on the other side of the mesa until the soldiers discovered and killed their friends below.

Another story, a latter day legend, is told by Maurine Parker Grammer in her Master's thesis (University of New Mexico, 1956) of the Eagle Dancers of San Ildefonso.

The Eagle Dance is a potent one in all the pueblos, assuring good harvests, sufficient rain, a beneficent season when properly performed. The flower of pueblo manhood is chosen to perform the dance, and the ritual cleansing of body, mind and heart must be strictly adhered to for four days prior to the dance.

In the time of the legend two young men were chosen to perform the dance, and in addition to the usual admonitions of the wise men of the pueblo, they were told in particular not to look upon two women with strange eyes who lived close to the base of Black Mesa.

The young men were overcome with curiosity on the night before the dance. They quietly crept out of the kiva and went to see what manner of women were these two who lived apart. They were welcomed,

BLACK MESA — View through the notch at top of the trail from San Ildefonso Pueblo

fed and entertained not only until the moon went down, but until the stars faded.

Silently they stole back to the kiva, and fearfully looked at the cloudy sky when they emerged for the dance. The gods were not happy, but the young men were loathe to tell of their disobedience.

When the drums called across the plaza, the young men, wearing the headdress and wings of the eagle, began to dance. Never had the oldest inhabitant seen the dance more beautifully executed.

Then the lithe brown hands of the drummers were stilled. The feet of the dancers had left the ground and they were dancing higher and higher in the gray morning air. Looking up, people saw two female eagles circling the plaza and soon the young men joined them and flew away over Black Mesa, never to return.

At San Ildefonso we were told yes, they knew the legend, but it happened at the Hopi pueblos, not here.

BUFFALO DANCE performed before San Ysidro church

# Never Plow on Sunday

*"Before a saint in Christian dress*
*I saw them dance their holiness,"*

Witter Bynner wrote of another Indian dance and another pueblo, Cochiti. But the words apply to Tesuque Pueblo, six miles north of Santa Fe; here the annual deer and buffalo dance is held before the little church dedicated to San Ysidro. (Also spelled San Isidro) Usually this dance is held on January 6, the "Little Christmas."

This legend is told, as many are, about several locations. There is a church at Agua Fria, just south of Santa Fe, dedicated to San Ysidro as well as many more scattered here and there where the patron saint is San Ysidro, the patron saint of farmers. Some say Tesuque, some say Agua Fria, some say other places as the site for this particular tale.

The legend tells of a farmer with a few acres and many children to feed. He grew frantic with the need to make the fields yield more food to nourish his growing brood. From day break to dark he labored, plowing and planting, and when Sunday came, instead of going to church, he went to the fields.

His good wife tearfully begged him to go to Mass but he would not. He was plowing, and oxen were slow, time short. He had work that must be done.

Fellow farmers, enroute to church, chided him. "Plow on Sunday and you will end up plowing for the Devil for all eternity," they told him. He shook his head and continued to plow.

Finally an angel in the form of a man came to the field to talk to him.

"This is the Sabbath, you must go to church," the angel said. "If you do not, God will send grasshoppers to eat your corn."

"Grasshoppers have come before, and doubtless will come again," the farmer said wiping sweat from his forehead with a ragged sleeve. "I must plow more land and plant more corn and beans so that some will be left for my family."

"If you do not go to church God will send rain to wash out the grain," the angel persisted, walking along by the farmer's side.

HORNO (outdoor oven) near church
of San Ysidro

SAN YSIDRO in church named
for him at Tesuque
— Photo by Holly Bond

"Of rain there is never enough in this land," the farmer answered. "I will welcome it!"

"Then God will send a drought to dry up your crops," threatened the angel.

"Drought I have had before," the farmer replied wearily. "Now I must plow."

"If you do not go to church," the angel insisted, "God will send you a bad neighbor. This neighbor will gossip about you, his dog will bite you, his cattle will break your fences."

The farmer really looked at the stranger for the first time, and dropped the reins he had held so tightly. Horror was in every line of his face. Quickly he ran across the furrows, paying no heed to his oxen, nothing except getting to church as quickly as possible.

At the church he pulled off his tattered hat and tip-toed his way to where his wife knelt and dropped on his knees at her side. His work-hardened hands reached out for her rosary and he softly began to recite his prayers. He could cope with anything but a bad neighbor. That he could not do.

When church was over and the people walked out into the sunlight, they were astonished to see the farmer's field all plowed. No one was more astonished than the farmer — this farmer called Ysidro. He became such a good and pious man that he is called a saint.

Little wooden statues of San Ysidro depict the farmer and the angel walking side by side, the angel holding the reins of the straining oxen as they plow the fields.

The Indians at Tesuque dance their ancient dances before the church dedicated to San Ysidro, only after they have attended Mass in the little chapel. They are farmers, tillers of the soil, and although some work in Santa Fe or at Los Alamos, none is a poor neighbor.

SAN YSIDRO church at Agua Fria

— Photo by Holly Bond

## *Pecos — The Feathered Serpent*

What do you think of when you hear the word *Pecos*? Is it a fishing trip to the river that rises in the Sangre de Cristo Mountains, twisting and rioting southward as the historic Pecos? Is it the tiny town some 27 miles southeast of Santa Fe? Or do your mental feet stir the nearby rich red and ocher dirt of the old Cicuye (Pecos) Pueblo ruins, which straddle a ridge along the river just off of Highway 85 as Pecos National Monument?

Today Park Service buildings are neatly arrayed at the base of the ridge, and a tall flag pole flies the stars and stripes. Picnic tables, trash containers and a drinking fountain attest to the American fetish of sight seeing in comfort. Gone are the matted buffalo hides, gone

RUINS of mission church at Pecos

MISSION CHURCH RUINS — View down hallway showing thickness of the walls

the ceremonial pots adorned with the feathered serpent and the rain-bird once shaped here. Sherds uncovered by wind and rain now mingle with those uncovered by archaeologists.

Rising stark against the almost daily thunderheads dominating the Pecos National Monument, is the ruin of the mission church of Nuestra Senora de los Angeles de Prociuncula, now being restored. The date of its construction is not exact, but is believed to be 1617. It was, according to historians, "a magnificent temple, adorned with six towers, three on each side, its walls so wide that services were held in their thickness."

In the strictest sense Cicuye (Pecos) was not really "discovered" by Coronado in 1540. His men were led to it. A delegation of Pecos Indians, led by two chiefs called Bigotes and Cacique by the Spaniards, arrived at Zuni pueblo while the Coronado party was still there. They

PECOS — Unusual layering of adobe bricks in mission church

had come to see what manner of men were these who walked in iron houses against which the strongest bow was powerless. They brought gifts — skins, shields, and their finest handwork. In return, they were given beads and a truly wondrous gift — bells.

Alvarado and some twenty men were sent by Coronado to visit Pecos. The pueblo was the largest they had seen, Alvarado reported, with houses four and five stories high, some very fine indeed, and there were eight large patios used by the 2,000 inhabitants.

If Bigotes told Alvarado (or Coronado when he later visited Pecos) about the feathered serpent, neither recorded it. But there are those who say the holy serpent still sleeps today in a hidden cave somewhere close to the old ruin, awaiting the return of his worshippers. There are even stories that say the feathered serpent is lethargic because it has been so long since he has been fed a pueblo virgin, even though there seems to be nothing in pueblo lore to indicate they practiced human sacrifice. The Spaniard was not interested in what the Indian believed so much as he was in teaching him Christianity.

Author Frank Applegate tells the story, as told to him by a Tewa Indian, that the Mexican Montezuma (or Moctezuma) was born in New Mexico at the old pueblo of Pose Uingge, twenty miles north of the present pueblo of San Juan. He "was born without a father like the Christian Jesus" and was not a particularly nice youth. He was then called Pose Ueve. He made friends with birds and animals, but

52

was lazy and wouldn't help his poor mother until the cacique (chief) died and a successor had to be chosen by lot. The choice fell on Pose, and he became a very good chief.

There were those at the pueblo who could not forget his former shiftless ways, and refused to honor him as his office demanded. Discouraged, Pose left and went to Pecos. Here he became a great cacique and changed his name to Montezuma.

So wise and good was Montezuma's rule at Pecos that even that great pueblo became crowded, and he decided to found other pueblos with the overflow. Before leaving Pecos, Montezuma lighted a fire on the altar of the sun. This fire was to be tended by twelve virgins, and the pueblo would prosper until his return.

Led by an eagle, Montezuma traveled southward, founding new homes for the pueblo peoples, and ultimately the great city of Mexico.

At Pecos, after many years, the virgins grew warm and sleepy one night, and the fire died as they slept. This was the beginning of the end for this once greatest of all the pueblos, say the legends.

Unlike the sacred fire, Pecos Pueblo died gradually. Where it had once been the trading site for plains and pueblo people, it weakened and became the victim of Apache and Comanche raids. Disease came in epidemic proportions — in 1768 smallpox wiped out all but 180 of these proud people. A few years later mountain fever left but a bit over half of their now scant number to mourn. When there were but 17 Pecos Indians left, in 1838, they reluctantly gave up and moved to Jemez.

The sacred fire no longer burned, Montezuma would not return. The hiss of the feathered serpent no longer answered the call of the drums – there were not enough dancers to perform the rites properly. Homes had fallen and only the lizard and Child of the Earth could find comfort in the rubble.

The restoration work being done today is on the mission church and convento, but a low stone wall that climbs and dips over the arroyos still guards the home site of a people that now live only in books and the tales told in winter at other pueblo firesides.

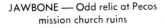
JAWBONE — Odd relic at Pecos mission church ruins

DORSEY ESTATE showing front gardens; photograph taken in the 1880's

# XII

*The Dorsey Mansion*
*East of Springer*

# A Gazebo, Gargoyles and Possibly A Ghost

Page Mr. Ripley! Here is one he missed — gargoyles, gazebos and ghosts rising out of rolling hills and grasslands 25 miles east of Springer, N. M. in the 36 room shattered elegance prosaically called "The Dorsey Mansion." Go see for yourself and you'll come away ready to believe anything so long as it is absolutely impossible.

Nothing about the Dorsey Mansion is believable except that it is there. Hand hewn hemlock beams in the basement, when hemlock came from either Washington state or Pennsylvania. A carved cherrywood staircase from England, leading from the parlor to the second floor. Mahogany woodwork; oak, walnut and hard maple flooring; fireplaces manteled and faced with blood onyx, marble and slate polished until it looks like marble. A walnut cathedral ceiling in the picture gallery ballroom; hardware from France on the doors; a 180 foot lily pond with built-in islands, one of which held a gazebo. The carved faces of the owner, wife and brother larger than life on a crenelated stone tower are completed with grinning gargoyles. All this was assembled and built when outland materials had to be freighted over the plains from St. Louis by wagon train!

Who did it? Don Turner in his "The Life and Castle of Stephen W. Dorsey" (Humbug Gulch Press) sums it up as "The hard working Vermont boy who became a Senator from Arkansas, a cattle baron in New Mexico and the key figure in a national political scandal."

Stephen Wallace Dorsey was all of that — and more. He was a man with a dream, one who fought his way from poverty in New England to being at least a partial president-maker. His energy and sweat congealed into what was called a Midas touch — railroads in Ohio, a huge cattle ranch in New Mexico — tinctured with political overtones as he became Senator from Arkansas, the key figure in the government's Star Mail route scandal, in which Dorsey was defended by infidel Robert G. Ingersoll.

He was acquitted (and built Ingersoll a home close by as a legal fee) but the long drawn-out trial was the beginning of Dorsey's financial ruin. Still he had founded three towns in New Mexico — Dorsey,

ART GALLERY and ballroom with cathedral
ceiling served later as post office

TOWER of mansion showing carved faces of
the Dorseys, surmounted by gargoyles

Chico, and Clayton. The first two are now ghost towns, the third a flourishing ranch and cattle center city. His only monument is the home he built, although Clayton was named for his son. When he died in Los Angeles in 1916 at the age of 74, the home he had built no longer was his; his cattle and the 24,000 acres had gone along with it.

The Civil War was over and the opportunities in the west were attracting an ever growing segment of people when Dorsey began to acquire his New Mexico land in Colfax County. The land centered around Chico Spring, which had been a camp site for wagon trains after rounding Point of Rocks (across the valley) on the Cimarron cutoff of the old Santa Fe Trail. That most precious of all liquids, water, was here and here he would build a home for himself and his beautiful wife, Helen. It would have every luxury the times boasted of, and the view would be fenced in only by the horizon.

The mansion began as a 22 room L-shaped structure. Logs were peeled for the outside walls, and oiled mountain mahogany and other hardwoods were used for interior woodwork.

The log structure was three stories high, with household servant quarters on the third floor. A study of early pictures reveals that the gabled windows on this floor were later additions. Unverified cost estimates are set at $50,000 — and this was in 1877! Whether this included the fabulous lily pond and gazebo is not known. This pond still exists, as does the house, and was built before the stone part of the mansion was constructed. It is 180 feet long and 40 feet wide, shaped roughly like a child's hobby horse laid on its side. Two "islands" were

CARRIAGE HOUSE awaits later restoration

STONE PORTION of house, currently occupied while restoration
work goes on in log section, which was built first

FOUNTAIN in garden pool, topped
by stone bobcat being
strangled by a snake

built in, one with a gazebo where the Dorseys and their guests could cool off on a warm summer day. Bridges connected the islands with the mainland.

The house was the social center for northern New Mexico. Elegant parties were held with guests coming in by buckboard and surrey from not only Springer, but Raton, Cimarron and Clayton. There were eastern guests, industrialists and politicians — the great and near great.

Soon the Dorseys felt the need for expanded space. Guests, coming so far, were quartered at the ranch, though parties often lasted all night. A pale red stone was available close by, and Dorsey brought a family of stone masons from Italy to construct the addition. It, too, is L-shaped, three stories high, with a full stone basement containing the steel-doored wine cellar, storage rooms, meat locker, etc.

Folk tales tell the story of a man either accidentally killed or murdered, and his body concealed behind the masonry here. He might account for still other local legends concerning two Mexican vaqueros hired to house-sit who fled in terror over ghostly manifestations and refused to return. The Deatons, now owners, have not been bothered since the first night they slept in the house, when what sounded like footsteps in the 75 foot second floor hall paced all night. Their dog, a friendly and well loved Heinz variety breed, still refuses to descend into the basement.

The stone section contains the tower, graced with sculptured faces of Dorsey, his wife Helen, and his brother. The faces are surmounted by traditional Renaissance gargoyles. One gargoyle, ugly as sin, reveals the likeness of Dorsey's hated rival, one Senator Blaine.

The stone addition is entered through a stained glass ornamented door and entrance way. It contains the fabulous cherrywood staircase rising from the parlor, the restored blood onyx fireplace, a dining room large enough to seat 50 guests, and the art gallery-ballroom with the lovely mahogany cathedral ceiling (later used as a post office). There are kitchens, butler's pantry, bedrooms — 14 rooms in all, plus the basement rooms. Restoration is well under way in this section by Mr. and Mrs. K. E. Deaton, the present owners.

The Deatons are, in their own way, as fabulous as Dorsey himself. They are the kind of middle class family you would love to have as neighbors. Deaton ran a filling station for 22 years, and Mrs. Deaton took care of the family, did prize winning needle work, painted in oil on china and canvas, and loved restoring beautiful old pieces of furniture.

They bought the Dorsey mansion and the 40 immediately surrounding acres in 1966 and took on what must be the biggest individual restoration job west of the Mississippi. Time, weather and neglect had made the Dorsey place a shambles, but room by room they are replastering, refinishing, restoring lovely woodwork, furniture, bric-a-brac — even a lot of things salvaged from the cistern. They are from Friona, Texas — not millionaires, but extraordinary people who love the grace and beauty that is here under fallen plaster and hideous coats of paint. They are doing with their own hands loving and skilled work and financing it by showing the mansion, for a modest fee to all who come. The mansion is open every day of the week and Sundays, all year round. It seems an impossible job until you see what they have accomplished; the Deatons are of the indomitable breed that gets things done against all odds.

Go see them — let them show you the big stone fountain (one of three in the front yard) topped by a savagely-biting bobcat encircled by a snake, with salamanders vainly crawling up the shaft to help in the frozen struggle. See the house, carriage house, the remains of the old greenhouse, the more than 70 buildings that once made this not only a mansion home, but a town called Chico.

Take the highway out of Springer to Abbott. Four miles beyond Abbott is a rest-recreation site, dominated by a huge power transformer station. A marked road at right angles leads 12 miles straight ahead to a low mesa. At the foot of this mesa is the old site of Chico and the Dorsey Mansion.

GRAN QUIVIRA — Church seen from pueblo site showing size of the rooms

# XIII

*Gran Quivira National Monument*

## *Gran Quivira!*

Gran Quivira — the very name spells wealth, romance, dreams. Gran Quivira, where household pots were made of gold, and tiny golden bells were hung in the trees to provide lulling music as vagrant breezes cooled the midday siesta for the dwellers in this mythical city.

It was the dream of finding this chimera that pulled Coronado (the man with the golden helmet) and his huge expedition northward into this new Mexico in 1540. His headquarters for two years was established near Bernalillo, N.M., and scouting parties ventured far — as far as what is now Rice County, Kansas. But they did not visit the Pueblo de Los Jumanos, the site that was to become honored, or saddled, with the name Gran Quivira.

He did not find the golden pots or tinkling bells. No Mexico City or room filled with gold to ransom their king as in Peru. The site now known as Gran Quivira was not visited by the pale, bearded ones until October of 1598, when Onate set out on a journey of discovery from his first European settlement north of Espanola at San Juan de los Caballeros. They traveled eastward to Pecos, then south into the Salinas province, on the other side of the Manzano Mountains bordering the Rio Grande. This was the first direct contact with Europeans for the Pueblo de los Jumanos.

In this first visit, the Spaniards demanded nothing. They were anxious to get on their way and locate the sea. It was different the next year, 1599, when one of Onate's men, Zaldivar and twenty five of his soldiers demanded mantas and provisions. The Jumanos gave them stones, and with such a small force with which to fight, Zaldivar retreated, but he did report what had happened.

A much larger force under Onate returned demanding a tribute of mantas. The Jumanos gave them twelve or fourteen which was all they had. Outraged the soldiers set fire to one corner of the pueblo the next day, fired upon the natives, killing several, and hanged two of the more vocal. In a disagreement over translation they then hung their own interpreter as well!

Two more major battles were fought during the next couple of years and the Indians lost, accepting the fact that the Spaniard would collect tribute levies of food and clothing from them, and the taking of some of their men to work on Spanish building projects and as servants. After one battle each Spanish soldier was given one Indian male as a servant.

It should be noted that the collection of levies from these Indians, struggling as they were to survive, was just as surely death as the sword; merely slower. They wept and cried out when collections were made, to no avail. Captain Velasco, in his report to the Viceroy in 1601 wrote:

". . . . I have seen and observed that the natives pick up the individual kernels of maize that fall to the ground; the Indian women will follow behind the loads for two leagues for this purpose."

There was no supermarket at the corner, no welfare system. A fanega of corn meant the difference between life and death. The Spaniard took what he wanted for himself and his horses.

The coming of the Mission Period meant little economically to the Indian of the Salinas. In return for the saving of his soul he was punished for his pagan beliefs; he gave up prime farming land to the support of the church, and contributed his labor to the building of great churches and conventos.

Among the most impressive ruins in these United States today are those of the mission churches at Gran Quivira, Quarai and Abo. Look at the towering walls that remain and imagine what it took, without tools, to build these buildings in the early 1600's!

ANCIENT CASTLE WALLS at Gran Quivira, as
impressive as a castle on the Rhine

BUILT TO LAST — Note thickness of wall seen through window

RUINS of Gran Quivira, with modern steps and railings

—Photo by Nelson Jay

WINDLASS used by treasure hunters at Gran Quivira

It was done, but it was too much. These people had not only to contend with the vagaries of weather and diseases, but the continued raids of their ancient enemies, the roving Indian tribes. By 1670 or shortly thereafter the exodus began. They left to find shelter and life itself with other Indians along the Rio Grande. The huge churches became the haunt of horny toads, lizards and rattlesnakes while salt-bush, cactus and yucca covered the mounded graves of their fallen homes.

Perhaps it was the impressiveness of these ruins that lent veri-similitude to fantastic stories of buried treasure at Gran Quivira — for these stories did originate and grow with the telling. Perhaps it was the name itself, though how the name became attached to this Pueblo de los Jumanos is unclear. The stories told of buried gold and silver from mines (what mines? there were none here) or rich church chalices, vessels, etc.

When Gran Quivira began to attract the attention of archaeo-logists they found the ruins pock marked with holes dug by treasure hunters. Perhaps the title of most colorful of these seekers goes to Count La Cerda.

Nina Otero Warren, in her book "Old Spain in Our Southwest," retells the story of La Cerda, who came to the Salinas area at the head of a band of Brazilian gypsies around 1900. It could be that the Brazilians thought of this as a chance to find a new life for themselves and their families, but La Cerda claimed he had an aunt in Spain who had ancient papers giving the location of thirty millions in treasure (including a one hundred pound diamond!), buried at Gran Quivira.

Before the "treasure" could be excavated, the Count became embroiled in a fight over a lovely senorita in Tajique and landed in jail when it was thought that he had killed a Mexican boy. The boy recovered and La Cerda's brother bailed him out of his troubles and took him back to Brazil. The brother testified that there was no Span-ish aunt, no treasure papers, but that instead La Cerda suffered from mental trouble.

Just as La Cerda is the most colorful, the members of the Yrisarri family were the most persistent. This family began the search, based on a chart scratched on a white stone, in the 1780's. It was passed on from son to grandson. Jacobo Yrisarri was "taken to Santa Fe and fined" in 1916 or 1917. He was sinking a shaft in the old San Isidro chapel site at Gran Quivira.

A permit to excavate for buried treasure was granted in 1930 to J. B. Wofford and Alfred J. Otero by Secretary of the Interior Harold Ickes — and it was Jacobo Yrisarri who supervised the dig-ging! This permit expired in 1933, and a new permit was denied. Jacobo faded from the scene, and one wonders where his white stone

CROSS in center of first chapel, where treasure hunters dug

ORIGINAL MANTEL at site of fireplace

map is today. The Park Service filled in his shaft and got rid of his debris in 1940. Preserved, that shaft and windlass might well be interesting to visitors at Gran Quivira today. It was, after all, a part of the history at this National Monument.

Gran Quivira can be reached from U.S. 60 by turning south at Mountainair and driving 26 miles on New Mexico 10. By careful use of time fairly nearby Quarai and Abo (both state monuments) may be inspected and photographed the same day as the Gran Quivira trip. If you are a shutter bug, you won't have film enough regardless of how many rolls you take along. Remember the Park Service slogan "Take nothing but pictures; leave nothing but footprints."

MISSION RUINS at Quarai, one of three
magnificent old churches in the Salinas

# The Blue Lady

Surely no more fantastic story has come out of any period of history in the new world than the legend of the Blue Lady. Legends there are in plenty, coming from Texas, New Mexico, Arizona and California about a woman, wearing the blue habit and veil of a nun, who always walked into Indian camps alone, healed the sick, taught Christianity, and walked away. Consistently, wherever the legends originate, she never stayed more than a few hours, never ate or drank water, and always told the natives that teachers (priests) would follow her to tell them of the Christian God, the Virgin Mary, and Jesus.

This, in itself, is incredible enough as an Indian legend of the 1600's. But when early mission priests, with no contact with each other, tell of Indians coming in to be baptized, saying that the Blue Lady sent them, then we really are in the middle of the fantastic.

In New Mexico we first hear about her through the Memorial of Fray Alonso de Benavides.

In 1621 the missions of New Mexico were formed into the "Custodia de la Conversion de San Pablo," with Fray Benavides as the first custodio. He relates the miraculous conversion of the Jumanos.

The people of the Salinas province, according to Benavides, kept asking for a padre to live among them. With so much territory to cover and so few padres to send, Benavides was slow in answering their request, but in 1629 he decided to send Fray Salas and Fray Diego Lopez back with the petitioners. Before assigning these priests he asked the Indians to tell him the reason they were so anxious for baptism.

The Indians told him that a woman like the one in the painting, (a miniature on the wall of his convento picturing Mother Louisa de Carrion,) preached to each tribe in its own tongue, telling them to summon the Fathers and "that they should not be slothful about it." They insisted that while the dress of the woman was the same, the face was not. Instead their visitor was young and beautiful. The picture of the nun, Luisa de Carrion, was the property of Fray Garcia de San Francisco y Zuniga, founder of the mission at Socorro, according to historian Ventancurt.

In 1531 Benavides was back in Spain, and still curious about the

QUARAI RUINS — Did the Blue Lady visit here?

strange woman who sent in the Indians. He visited a young and beautiful nun by the name of Maria de Jesus (Maria de Agreda) of the town of Agreda in the province of Soria, Spain. Here he heard from her own lips of her marvelous "flights" to New Mexico, where she had conversed with the Indians in their own languages although she knew not a word of them excepting while on the spot.

Historically Maria de Jesus was born in 1602 and died in 1665. Her family name was Coronel. She had entered the Convent of the Immaculate Conception at Agreda in 1619, as did her mother at the same time. Her father and two brothers immediately made it a family affair by becoming Franciscan friars.

In the two weeks that Benavides spent in Agreda, Maria de Jesus, now Mother Superior at the convent, described baptisms and details in far away New Mexico that only he, Benavides, knew. She said that she had been present on these occasions, that the Indians could see her, but the Europeans could not.

Certain it is that Maria had never left the convent, much less Spain. She made her "flights" sometimes three or four in a day's time, while resting on her hard bed in the convent!

Had New Mexico been her only point of visitation one might suspect that someone, somehow, had told her about the Salinas province. But the legends are far too widespread.

Don Damien Manzanet, in writing a letter relative to the discovery

JUMANOS who lived here were sent by the Blue Lady
to be baptized as Christians

ABO MISSION could seat five hundred and boasted
an organ — in the mid-1600's!

of Matagorda Bay, Texas (1689) tells of the Blue Lady there. He had an Indian governor come to him wanting BLUE cloth for a burial shroud for his mother when she died. On being questioned as to his demand for blue (nothing else would do) the Indian told Manzanet that before his time the Lady in Blue had often visited his tribe. His mother remembered her well, as did many of the old ones, he said, and he wanted to have the blue the lady wore for his mother's burial shroud.

The padres of the San Agustin mission wrote in 1668 of the Blue

Lady's visits among the Indians there; French explorer St. Denis wrote in 1710 of the Indian legends of her visits.

Legends in Arizona tell of her healing a sick chieftain's son — and in California frightened warriors were said to have shot arrows through her which hurt her not, for she continued to advance. Other legends, widely separated geographically, tell of Indians who knew the Crucifix because of what the Blue Lady had told them.

In 1631 Maria de Jesus wrote out her account of her visitations, at which time they are supposed to have ceased because of church disapproval — but the stories go on and on.

A little girl, lost on the Texas plains, was led to a deserted church, and when found three days later was neither hungry or thirsty. The beautiful lady in the long blue dress had led her there, and taken care of her. No such person could be located. The child's description of the dress was clearly that of a nun's habit, including the veil.

In the Salinas region of New Mexico, where the Blue Lady legend for New Mexico persists, are three church ruins that are the most imposing in these United States. They are Gran Quivira, Quarai and Abo. Whether these Indians were more receptive to Christianization because of visits from the Blue Lady cannot be determined at this late date, but we know that Fray Benavides thought so.

Occasionally one will hear that the Indian and Spanish custom of painting window facings and doors "Taos" blue goes back to the Blue Lady. This would be hard to pin down, if indeed it were true, because Taos blue is the color of the revered turquoise, beloved by all Indian tribes in the southwest. One plump, kindly Indian matron answered the query of, "Why blue?" very succinctly. "It's pretty," she said, and turned back to her task of painting her door blue.

SHADOWS OF THE PAST — Sturdy walls at Gran Quivira

# The Legend of San Jose

Legends, like parables, carry a truth of their own that is difficult to transmit in any other way. New Mexico is rich in legend, folklore, call it what you will, blending as it does three cultures, Indian, Spanish and Anglo. The legends sometimes embody more than one culture.

The story of San Jose at Cienega, a little village some fourteen miles south of Santa Fe, is characteristic and hauntingly lovely. Actually we have three with one underlying theme, all centered in the five-foot statue of San Jose, staff in his right hand, his left arm protectively cradling the Infant Jesus. Both wear crowns of gold.

San Jose is the patron saint of Cienega, and the story is told that the statue was brought to the valley shortly after the reconquest by an early-day priest, Father Joseph. A church had not yet been built but a rico — a wealthy land owner — offered Father Joseph the hospitality of his hacienda, and opened his private chapel not only for the padre and the statue, but for all the people of the community. As the years tread upon each other's heels, the padre grew old and sick unto death.

"San Jose belongs to the village," he told the people. "It is to remain here always."

The good padre died, and eventually the rico died too, and his estate, after the manner of the times, was divided among his children.

A son, grown to manhood with the statue of San Jose in the family chapel which was a part of his inheritance, decided to move to land he owned near Algodones. A new hacienda had been built there, and a chapel for San Jose. Ox carts were piled high with household goods, and one was padded with soft rugs and blankets to carry the statue. The journey was begun, but the cart carrying San Jose moved ever more slowly, as though weighted with more than the oxen could pull.

Drivers flayed the oxen to no avail, and finally the oxen dropped dead from the strain before the cart had left the village fields behind. While drivers went for more oxen, people working in the fields gathered around the cart to see what manner of freight it carried to sink the big wooden wheels hub deep into the hard packed road. It was San Jose!

"San Jose belongs to us!" they protested. "He cannot be taken

SAN JOSE holding the infant, Jesus. Note the gold crowns

away." Quickly they ran to a nearby rancho and borrowed a cot. Reverently they lifted the now very light statue and put it on the cot, carried easily by two men. Each step back toward the village the image became lighter. San Jose did not want to leave this parish. Thus it is that He remains in the village to this day.

A variation of the legend of the good San Jose is that at one time evil men, believing that gold had been hidden inside the statue, attempted to steal it and carry it away. They were no more successful than the son of the rico had been. Less than half a mile from the chapel the image became so heavy it could not be moved and they were

TREES dedicated to San Jose border site of
the original church at Cienega

forced to leave Him on the road while they fled the wrath of the parishioners, wiser if not better men.

A third variation of the story concerns the site of the church. The old chapel had been at the far end of the village, on the land now being farmed by the Tapia family. This small canyon site has been dammed up as a family pond to store water for irrigation and only a few yards of back foundation stone rises above the reed and water plants choking the pond. Building a church was important, and at the lower end of the valley the farmers wanted it there.

There were quite a number of people living in the area at the

PRESENT CHURCH of Cienega, and composanto which
lies between it and site of an older church

northern end of the valley, where the Simms Ranch is now located, and
these people wanted the church built near them. For a time it seemed
they might have their wish, and since the old chapel was leaking badly,
San Jose was carried to the center of the valley for protection until a
church could be built.

When parishioners, carrying their precious statue, arrived at a
spot just south of the present church site, the image grew very heavy
— too heavy to move on. This was the spot, the weight seemed to say,
where the church was to be built. It was done.

This chapel, too, deteriorated with time and when heavy rains not
only stained the walls, but one wall began to crumble, it was decided
not to try to repair, but to build a new chapel just across the camposanto
(cemetery) from the old location. This chapel is the one that is in use
today.

A special niche was built just back of the altar for San Jose, and He is happy there.

Mrs. Henry (Melinda) Gonzales, born in Cienega, remembers that as a girl the women vied with each other to make their hand stitchery fine enough for the robes in which they dressed the image. Today His robes are painted, but the Infant Jesus still is dressed with the most exquisite of fabrics and the finest seamstress' lovingly stitch the garments the Infant wears.

Fresh flowers are renewed frequently at the base of the statue, and gifts of thankfulness for the answer to prayers are reverently left for San Jose and His church. The Holy Infant once wore a tiny gold wrist watch, patently a gift by an unknown parishioner in gratitude — a variation of the widow's mite. At one time, too, the hair worn by San Jose was from the head of a young girl, given because she had pledged her shining glory if she recovered from a serious illness. This same maiden later became a nun, entering a teaching sister order.

The Church of San Jose in Cienega today is small, meticulously clean, the pastel-colored windows shedding soft light inward during the daylight hours and at night, when the church is lighted, sending out delicately tinted fingers of light inviting the community and stray visitors to join in the worship.

RUINS of turquoise mining buildings
and headframe of a deep, dangerous shaft

# XVI

# Skystone of Los Cerrillos

A president of these United States is said to have remarked, when told that the then fledgling Smithsonian Institution was trying to obtain specimens of stone fallen from the sky (meteorites), "I would rather believe these gentlemen were fools than liars."

The Indian, wandering over Mt. Chalchuitl in the Cerrillos area, or perhaps the Burro Mountains near Silver City, some two thousand years ago (give or take a hundred years or so) wasn't bothered with the "knowledge" that stones could not possibly fall from the sky. That lovely piece of outcropping rock there by the pinon tree had to have fallen from the sky. It was the color of the sky, a beautiful deep blue. We call that stone turquoise.

Man's mental processes are not perturbed by the color of his skin, and the Indian also wove stories to account for things he did not understand. Of course there are legends to account for the sometimes clear blue stone (male turquoise) or the greenish (female) turquoise that the Indians continued to find and then to search for earnestly. Sometimes the wondrous stones were considered the bones of one of the Hero Twin Gods accidentally killed by his brother. That didn't stop the Indian from learning to use stone adzes and stone mauls to tear the skystone from its rocky bed. Sometimes he said that it wasn't the bones of the Hero Twin, but the heart of his mother. When she saw her son slain, her heart burst with such force that the fragments (turquoise) were forced deep into the earth in New Mexico, Colorado, Nevada, Arizona and Utah, as well as just over the state line in California.

Somewhere along the way, perhaps because he built a fire to keep warm (close up against a turquoise bearing ledge), he found that heat, particularly when followed by a pot of cold water, shattered the rocky matrix in which the turquoise was embedded. This trick made the mining of turquoise a bit easier, so he used it.

From the open pit, where without metal tools he tore away the blanket of earth, the Indian progressed to narrow shafts and inclined passages back into mountain sides, and eventually to winzes (passages from one level to another). Without animal or mechanical

CERRILLOS DAY attracts crowds to the town
famous for early-day turquoise mines

transportation aids, the separating of the skystone from the matrix
called for the lapidary shop to be at the mine itself, or very close
by.

To get from one level inside the mine to another, he usually used
chicken ladders — i. e. notched logs, and carried his raw treasure out
in baskets, held to his shoulders by headbands. The lapidary shop
outside used deer and elk horn, bits of bone, fire pointed wood or
turtle shell to pick the turquoise from the stone. With sandstone and
sweat he removed excess matrix. Today it is easier to get the matrix
from the mine, but no one has yet found a better way to get turquoise
out of the matrix than the way the Indian did it — by hand.

Turquoise mines of Indian origin are dotted around the southwest. One of the oldest is at Los Cerrillos (the little hills), 23 miles
southeast of Santa Fe on State Highway 10. Even before they arrived
in this area, Spaniards knew about the turquoise. Cabeza de Vaca
told of Opata Indians giving him turquoise. Estevan, the blackamoor
who had been with de Vaca and who preceded Friar Marcos de
Niza into New Mexico, was the first on-the-spot European collector
of the sky stone, but there wasn't as much of it as he reported!

That the Indian considered the turquoise powerful magic is
indisputable from the findings by archaeologists — in burials, under
kiva supports, in his arts and crafts. His legends and myths are even

more emphatic. He wore or carried it for protection from everything from snakes and lightning to witchcraft. A tiny flake of it under a laboriously built house would keep that wall from falling. A changing of color in his wife's turquoise was a sign of adultery!

The turquoise mines at Cerrillos are said to have been a potent contributing factor in the Pueblo Indian Rebellion of 1680. The legend states that the Spaniards were working the mines with Indian slave labor. This mine dates back to about 500 A.D. and modern experts estimate that at least 100,000 tons of rock were moved out of the mine BEFORE the Spaniard arrived. There was, again the legend, a very bad cavein, killing many Indians.

That Indians were killed in cave-ins is certain — whether in their own operations or under the Spaniard. The bones have been un-covered in modern operations.

In 1881 a geologist by the name of J. B. Hyde sank two shafts into Mt. Chalchuitl in the Cerrillos area, planning to work the hill for gold, silver and turquoise. During this unsuccessful operation he found two caves which had been worked centuries earlier and sealed off by the Indians. He dubbed the caves Wonder and Mystery. A number of artifacts were retrieved. Though the caves were dry when reopened, there was evidence that they had once been flooded by seepage. A "canoe" — actually a sort of raft, used in transporting men and ore over the water to the far side, was still there in 1870, according to a report by F. A. Jones of the United States Geological Survey.

Several owners after Hyde led up to the American Turquoise Company, who operated the mine until 1910. Governor Otero gave the figure of $1,600,000 as the worth of turquoise extracted from these mines between 1891 and 1896. The title had long since passed from Indian hands, but the Santo Domingo Indians still claimed it. Cochiti Indians unsuccessfully attempted to go in and mine tur-quoise during the last years of the 19th century.

Whether the great jewelry firm of Tiffany ever really owned the mine at Cerrillos known as the Tiffany is a matter of dispute. They did pronounce the turquoise from Cerrillos as the best and purest in the world, including the Persian deposits in their rating.

The Indian has lost none of his love for the skystone. His tur-quoise and silver jewelry is his status symbol in a much more realistic way than the Anglo's ranch style home or his Cadillac at the curb. For festive affairs (dances, Gallup Intertribal, et al) his jewelry is worn proudly, and if he does not feel he has enough for very impor-tant events, he will borrow from kinsmen.

Shops throughout the southwest display and sell turquoise and silver Indian jewelry. Southwesterners (and others) do not have to be Indian to love it. Old bits are quite expensive now, and hard to come by, but the modern jewelry is beautiful and relatively inexpensive. Tiny flakes are still used to adorn prayer plumes and other ceremonial regalia, for whether it be religious, social or economic, turquoise still has great significance.

Cerrillos is a fun place to visit. The town is completely Old West — it has even been used as a movie set! The old Tiffany Saloon serves gourmet food at reasonable prices.

STONE FLUME (?) left from
mining operations leads from
hilltop to valley floor

# XVII

## *Fray Padilla — The Coffin That Raises*

The Indian Pueblo of Isleta, thirteen miles south of Albuquerque, traditionally has been a place of refuge for troubled living spirits. When raiding Apaches, Utes, Navajos, disease and drought beset the Saline Pueblos, across the Manzano Mountains from Isleta, many of these sick and hungry people migrated to Isleta. So, too, when the Rebellion of 1680 drove the Spaniard from New Mexico, Isleta gave the fleeing colonists refuge, and many Isletans journeyed south with the retreating Iberians to build Isleta del Sur, near El Paso.

But for one padre, buried in the Mission church of San Antonio de Isleta, there has not been undisturbed peace. His coffin, a hollowed-out cottonwood log, surfaces not just in legend but in historical fact. Tradition and history agree that it is the coffin of Fray Padilla — but which Fray Padilla?

One version of the story says that this is the coffin of Fray Francisco Padilla, who accompanied Coronado in the expedition of 1540. History tells us that this good padre elected to remain and work with the Indians when Coronado traveled back to Mexico in 1542. Oral history has it that he was martyred soon after Coronado left; certainly there is nothing to tell what became of him if indeed he did not die a martyr, and soon.

Legend has it that he was indeed slain, and his body concealed in a hollowed-out cottonwood log. Strangely the body did not decompose and the plains Indians carried it out of their area back into the caves of the Pueblo country, where it remained secreted until after the Pueblo Rebellion of 1680, when the Mission of San Antonio (first built in 1613) was restored. The cottonwood log was carried to the church and there interred near the altar. It did not, however, stay at the level it was buried, but rose to the surface of the hard-packed earthen floor of the mission. Stories whispered say that the body was strangely flexible, that the arms could be bent easily. The death-dealing wounds were clearly discernable on the left side of the skull just below the ear. An all night wake was held, and the coffin was reburied in the same spot.

A second story of Fray Padilla is that the body is that of Fray Juan J. Padilla who was assigned to the Mission in Laguna Pueblo in 1733.

MISSION CHURCH at Isleta Pueblo where Fray Padilla is buried

Life in this frontier country was not easy for anyone at that time, and the priest had to minister to a wide territory.

One winter day, some years later, Fray Padilla was called to administer the last rites to a dying parishioner. As he mounted his horse to return home, snow was flying thickly, so heavily that he lost his way.

Cold, tired, hungry and lost, he was indeed happy to see through the swirling flakes a misty lamplight through the window of a small adobe house. He stopped to ask directions and warm himself at the fireplace.

His knocking brought a lone woman to the door. Recognizing the good padre she made him welcome and quickly prepared a hot meal for him. She was the wife of a Mexican gambler.

As Fray Padilla ate, the gambler returned home — drunk and angry, for on this day he had lost heavily at the games. Seeing the padre, he did not pause to question, but immediately attacked and killed the priest.

As the poor woman sobbed "El padre! el padre!" the drunken man slowly realized what he had done, and feared the consequences. He carried the priest out to his horse, tied the body securely into the saddle, looped the bridle reins over the saddle horn and slapped the horse's rump to send him galloping off into the storm.

When morning dawned, bright and clear, early risers at Isleta saw the horse standing patiently at a corral gate, still bearing its dreadful burden, the slain priest.

Fray Padilla was buried, as was the custom of the time, in the church. "But with such a death, how could he rest well?" the Indians say. Burial records at Isleta show "Juan J. Padilla, killed by stabbing thrusts."

How many times the coffin has surfaced is unclear, but tradition has it about once in every twenty years. A dramatic episode on December 24, 1889 eventually led to an investigation by the Catholic Church.

On this Christmas eve the Indians, without the knowledge or permission of the priest, decided to hold an Indian dance in the church. As the drums throbbed a strange pounding was heard, the altar itself swayed, and the coffin surfaced.

An excellent account of the investigation, which did not take place until April 25, 1895 is given by Julia Keleher and Elsie Ruth Chant in their book "The Padre of Isleta," the story of Father Anton Docher at the pueblo.

Father Docher participated in the investigation, conducted by "His Highness, the Bishop of Santa Fe, Most Reverend Placido Luis Chapelle, into the remains of Reverend Francisco Padilla, who had been killed by the Indians of Quivira, according to the tradition three hundred fifty years before."

The coffin was exhumed, from the very spot tradition had placed it, and the lid was lifted. The body was now mummified and there was no flexibility. Over the neck was a purple stole in a well preserved condition.

Testimony was taken from elder natives who had witnessed prior risings of the coffin, and a physician, Dr. W. R. Tipton, was present to write a report on the condition of the corpse. Now, however, one foot was missing.

When the investigation was over, the body was reburied in the same coffin at the same place. This time interred with it was a small metal box containing the findings of the investigation and signatures of the participants. There was nothing to clarify why the coffin raises.

Fray Angelico Chavez, a meticulous researcher, notes that an investigation was made in 1819, under the Franciscan Custos, Fray Francisco de Hozio (El Palacio, November 1947), thus predating the 1895 investigation by three quarters of a century. This investigation was overlooked when the later one was held.

A floor has been put in the church now, and if Fray Padilla's coffin breaks the earth, it will not be so readily seen. Scientists say that it is the shifting of the sand here on the river bed where the mission stands that forces the coffin to the surface. The Indians shrug. If this one, why not the others? They do not rise, and many are the burials in the church and in the camposanto just outside.

BUTTRESSED WALLS of Isleta Mission
ISLETA PUEBLO doorway by Mission

An additional legend has grown out of the opening of the Fray Padilla coffin in 1895. Father Docher, so well beloved at Isleta, took part in this investigation. Soon after, his hand and arms swelled and turned black. The people say, "with his own hand he found the wound that had caused the death of the early churchman and white worms were there. One bit him."

Realists say that the priest ran a splinter of bone in his finger and infection set in. Doctors said the infected arm had to come off, but Father Docher knelt before the altar and promised a novena of masses each year for Fray Padilla if the infection would leave him. It did.

Father Docher died December 18, 1928, and he, too, is buried before the altar at Isleta.

History, legend, tradition interwoven.

HISTORIC CHURCH at Acoma Pueblo as it is today

# XVIII

*Acoma Pueblo*

## Enchanted Mesa and The Sky City

Long before the coming of the white man, tradition has it that Acoma Indians lived on Enchanted Mesa, or Katzimo, their name for the site. Far across the seas, about which they knew nothing, castles were built surrounded by moats with drawbridges for protection. Here nature had fashioned for them mesas with sheer walls of living stone higher than any castle wall built.

Atop these mesas, homes could be more easily defended. They had need of protection because wandering bands of Comanche, Apache, Navajo and Utes often raided the pueblos for their stores of food, taking their women and children as slaves, killing the men.

Katzimo was an ideal home site. There was only one way the heights could be scaled; a stone monolith stood very close by the mesa. This ladder stone was close enough that gouged out toe holes could be supplanted with ladder rungs, narrow enough that it could be climbed single file only, and thus easily defended.

Standing alone, Katzimo was surrounded by fields where corn, beans and squash could be planted, and the harvest carried to the impregnable heights. The gods were good, and the people happy.

So safe and happy that they grew lax in their religious rites. Busy and content, dances were not danced as they should have been, and the young did not learn the rituals precisely. The sun father and earth mother continued to supply their needs until one fateful day.

It was the harvest season, and corn ears were plump, crops hung heavy on the vines, ripened in the sun. Everyone in the pueblo was gathering the crops except three women who were ill and a young boy, left to care for them. Then the penalty for their neglect struck.

The thunderbird, flying overhead, shook his wings in anger. The lake on his back spilled water the like of which no living man had ever seen. In the fields the people huddled together with their backs to the torrent but on Katzimo the homes were endangered. Water washed at foundations, penetrated the roofs and nibbled ceaselessly at walls.

"Go for the men," the women told the boy "Without them the houses will fall!"

The boy obeyed, and descended the ladder in rain much like a waterfall. He had gone but a short distance toward the fields when the earth beneath his feet seemed to tremble in anger, and a rumbling crash sounded in his ears. The ladder rock, undermined by flood waters, had fallen!

As swiftly as it had come, the rain was gone, but so was the only way to ascend the mesa. The people gathered at the mesa base and gazed upward where the three women, their illness forgotten in the greater

QUIET STREETS in the ancient Sky City

tragedy, ran along the mesa rim, wailing for help. None could be given. Frantically the men tried to climb, uselessly. Their protection was now their enemy. The sheer rock walls could not be climbed. They were homeless.

The three women were helpless. As day followed agonizing day, one jumped to try to join her husband and children far below. They buried her where she struck.

Sorrowfully they looked around them. There was one mesa, a mile away, that could be scaled if toe holds were cut. They cut them and began the slow business of building new homes on this mesa. These homes still endure, known to all men as Acoma, the Sky City.

When food and water gave out on Katzimo, the two women died, but when the cold winds of winter blow, their cries are still heard, so it is said, from the now barren top of Katzimo.

Building the new pueblo was not easy. Today there is a steep road built in 1941 when Walter Wanger filmed "Sundown" on the mesa. The old toe-hold trail is still in use, and you may climb it if you wish.

When the Spaniards came, Acoma was well established in the new location. Three-story houses had been built, with every bit of soil for mortar and abode carried up the precarious trail to the top of the mesa. The Acoma people were suspicious of these strangers who wore armor that threw back the lances of the sun; the intruders were frightening people who walked on four legs like the buffalo, but some of them walked as men walk, on two legs. They carried sticks that spoke with the voice of the thunderbird and delivered death as does the lightning when it strikes the high mesa tops. Were these new gods? Acoma had not forgotten what happens when gods are angry.

Some of the warriors descended to the plains, carrying gifts of skins of deer and buffalo, fowl, pinon nuts and other food for Coronado and his men. This was in December of 1540. Coronado himself climbed the path to Acoma (Acuco), and even this intrepid explorer was awed by its impregnable position.

When Onate brought the first settlers to this new Mexico in 1598, he too visited Acoma, as did his followers, the Zaldivars, Don Vicente and Don Juan. Don Juan Zaldivar, beguiled by the apparent friendliness of the Acoma chief Zutucapan allowed his small contingent of soldiers to become separated, and paid with his life. Onate did not dare let the death of his men go unpunished — the Indians were already becoming aware that the Spaniards were mortal! He sent Don Vicente, brother of the slain Don Juan to punish the Acoma Indians. Don Vicente was able, in a fierce battle in 1599, to kill 500 of the Acomas and to destroy the major part of their village.

Acoma patiently rebuilt the village, but there was no love for the

ENCHANTED MESA near Acoma Pueblo

HIGH WALLS of Acoma are aged by centuries

bearded ones. In 1629 Father Juan Ramirez, hearing of this fiercest of villages, asked to be assigned to it.

Legend says he ascended the path with no protection other than his breviary and his cross, and though enough arrows were loosed to kill a dozen, not one entered his habit. The Indians were bewildered and impressed.

During the ascent an eight year old Acoma girl fell from the cliff top to some rocks 60 feet below. Father Ramirez went to her, knelt and prayed over her, and led her unharmed up the cliff. The Indians deemed this a miracle and accepted him. He stayed on in the Sky City, and it was he who supervised the building of the church — San Estevan. (1629-1640). The timbers in the original church (some still remain) were carried from the holy mountain of the Indian world, 30 miles away, on the bare backs of the Indians.

The church was badly damaged in the Rebellion of 1680, and the padre, Father Louis Maldonado, was killed. The church was rebuilt in 1699.

Stories of voices and hauntings in the convento adjoining the church are sometimes told when the old ones talk of the times that went before. Doors slam when there is no wind, slam so hard that hinges are damaged. Could it be Padre Maldonado still seeking to escape?

The rose and buff cliffs of Katzimo seem very close as one stands on Acoma today in bright sunlight — but when moon shadows grotesquely sprawl across the lonesome land below, it is easy to hear, in the eerie night, sounds that might be the rustle of the wings of the thunderbird. But do not be too sure that the long drawn wail of a coyote is indeed coyote.

PLUMBING FACILITIES are not exactly modern

92

LAGUNA MISSION church showing the bell tower

# XIX

*Laguna Pueblo*

## The Magic Painting

Laguna is a small Indian Pueblo just off of Highway 66 (Interstate 40), about 46 miles west of Albuquerque. The word "laguna" means "lake" in Spanish, while the Indians themselves called it "Pokwindiwe oneur — pueblo by the lake." The original lake bed is now a meadow.

The Laguna land grant was issued in 1689 by the King of Spain, though the village as it now exists was not built until toward the close of the 18th century, beginning high up on the hill and spilling down into the valley.

Laguna Indians are Keres stock, probably originally from Acoma, when the Sky City became overcrowded and the fields had to be planted farther and farther from that penol. There was some absorption of peoples from Zuni, Zia and perhaps other nearby pueblos. That a relationship existed between Acoma and Laguna leads to the true story of the ownership of a painting that United States courts were called upon to decide — not because of money value, but for the legendary power it was felt to possess.

The painting hangs today in the church at Acoma, a painting of

San Jose (St. Joseph) so old and dim that it is difficult to see more than dim outlines. No photographing is permitted inside the church, and even if it were, a photograph of the San Jose painting would be of little value, so dim is the original.

Tradition has it that the painting was brought to Acoma by Fray Ramirez, the first padre to be stationed permanently at the pueblo. Fray Ramirez is the padre who built the original church there. Many of the Indians in both pueblos feel that the spirit of Fray Ramirez remains in this bit of canvas and oil.

In the late 1700's, the crops at Laguna were consistently poorer than those at Acoma, say the old tales. Laguna felt that it was because Acoma had the painting and thus the blessing of Fray Ramirez. Whether they borrowed or stole the painting is unknown, or indeed what happened at all.

HAND CARVED DOORS of mission church at Laguna

OLD WALLS of Laguna still stand

At any rate, in the early 1800's, with the painting at Laguna, the crop situation reversed. Now Laguna had good yields and Acoma poor ones. Whether it was because possession of the precious canvas enabled the holders to water fields with more sweat and consistency cannot be determined, or mayhap the blessing really was there.

The Acoma people came to reclaim their painting, and were repulsed by armed guards. The Laguna chapel was guarded day and night to protect the magic talisman. Eventually bad times at Acoma became so severe that its people were determined to fight to recover the canvas.

Father Lopez was in charge of both churches, and seeking to avert armed conflict, he suggested a possible solution. A number of slips of paper would be placed in a basket, one slip only to bear the likeness of San Jose.

The basket would be placed at the feet of the saint, and after a Mass, single representatives chosen by the people of each pueblo would draw until one drew the slip with the saint. Since this would be in church, and following a Mass, the result would be a divine decision.

Both pueblos agreed. Since this was so important, it is easy to imagine how fervently Indians at both pueblos prayed for the decision to favor them. Perhaps, too, prayer plumes were planted to secure the help of Indian gods. For the Indian believing in God in all things, there is no inconsistency in supplicating with prayer plumes, dancing, Mass and rosary.

HORNO (oven) beside a Laguna street

At last the great day of decision dawned. Father Lopez was selected to represent Acoma and a Laguna maiden called Margarite represented her people.

Father Lopez drew the first ballot — blank. With trembling hand Margarite drew one. Blank. Thus it went until Father Lopez abstracted the fifth slip from the basket — and there was St. Joseph. By lot the painting belonged to Acoma.

The happiness of Acoma was too short lived to be tasted. Laguna refused to yield possession of the treasure. The bitterness, if anything, was increased.

Meanwhile General Kearney raised the flag of the United States over the territory of New Mexico. Father Lopez now suggested that ownership of the painting be ruled upon by the civil authorities. It has been said that every cent the Indians could gather went to pay attorneys — and Acoma vs. Laguna went to district court, then on to the territorial Supreme Court in January, 1857.

The decision of the court gave the painting to Acoma. Jubiliantly they started for Laguna to claim it. Half way there, at the side of the trail, they found the painting propped up against a pinon tree.

Acoma says St. Joseph was so happy to come back to them that he came half way to meet them. It seems more probable that the Laguna people did not want to witness the triumphs of their opponents.

It might be, too, that they remembered an old legend of their people. This legend says that a cacique (chief) of Laguna had a vision prior to the coming of the Spaniard.

In this revelation the cacique was told of the coming of the pale-skins. He was warned that if the Lagunans were to adopt the customs of these people, with their "hard shoes and soft food" it would result in ill for the Indians.

Just as Acoma did not give up hope while the painting was at Laguna, Laguna continues to hope and seek legal means for regaining it. From the sidelines there would seem to be substantial merit to the claims of the Lagunas as well as to the claims of the Acomas.

OLD MISSION church of Laguna seen from highway

# XX

# Witches in the Oldest House

We Americans are prone to be the suffix "-est" people. The highest, the longest, newest, oldest, widest, tallest, anything but modest. Santa Fe has its share of the tendency. The oldest capital city in these United States with, naturally, the oldest government house (El Palacio, the Mud Palace), the oldest church (San Miguel) and the oldest house.

Let's explore legends of the oldest house. Standing together — there is only a very narrow one-way street between them — the house is even more "est" than San Miguel church.

Nineteenth century pictures show the house with two stories, though now there is only one. Tourists and natives see the old vigas (beams) which are scaley, cracked and sagging with age, but still there. How old is the house?

No one really knows. Legend has it that it was once the home of the Indian chief who ruled over Montezuma's northern empire. That empire had fallen before Coronado and his men made their way up the Rio Grande in 1540, but the house was there, an old one even then. Some there are who say it antedates the coming of Coronado by at least a century, basing the contention on construction details and bits of pottery found in the immediate area.

When the capitol was moved from up north in the Espanola Valley, San Juan de los Caballeros and San Gabriel, down to the site that is now Santa Fe (between 1609 and 1612) the oldest house was assigned to the Indian slaves. The Spaniard had a fair share of them, some brought from the south with Onate, some garnered along the way.

Standing there in the sun, the house watched the building of El Palacio across the river and San Miguel Chapel next door. When the turbulent and bloody Indian revolt came in 1680, it watched the burning and partial destruction of buildings the Spaniard had erected, and the retreat to the south from whence the intruders had come. There are no signs that the Indians attempted the destruction of these

OLDEST HOUSE as seen in Santa Fe today

OLDEST HOUSE as pictured in 1889 in Harper's Weekly

old slave quarters, possibly because they were Indian made, not the work of the conqueror.

The old house could watch the Indians bathing in the river, lathering liberally with the age-old amole, yucca root, to wash away every taint of the Spaniard and his religion. And the house was there, still sunning itself, when De Vargas retook the city in 1692. Originally there must have been at least a few other dwellings for company, if legend be true, for it was said to have been a part of the old pueblo Kaw-Pu-Gee, place of the mussel shell people.

The oldest house has been the home of many. There is one story that a Franciscan padre occupied it, and as close as it is to San Miguel Chapel this might well have been so. Whether a good padre lived there or not, as late as 1880 four families lived in it, complete with kids and chickens.

The most exciting residents ascribed to the old house by the tellers of tales are two very powerful brujas (witches) in the 1800's. They were at least part Indian, and their spells and magic were considered extremely potent. When night blanketed the city, some of the ruling politicians and very pious residents lifted the latch on the wooden door to consult with these women and to buy their potions. They could supply charms and drugs to make certain that an erring husband not only returned to his own fireside, but hated the charmer who had lured him away. A tiny bit of personal finery of a young senorita, a snippet of hair or finger nail paring delivered to the brujas could be used in a concoction to cause her to find the suitor completely irresistable. A hated rival, in love or business, could be made to sicken and die.

A macabre bit comes from this period, during the tenure of the brujas. It seems that *two* swains, each eager for the hand of one certain lovely girl, consulted the brujas separately. One won her love, and the disappointed suitor stormed the brujas for the return of his gold pieces. They refused a refund. In his anger and frustration, he struck out at one of them. The other bruja grabbed a big hunting knife and swung at the fiery young Spaniard so viciously that his head was severed from his body.

On the anniversary of his death each year, say the tales told in the firelight, his head rolls down College Street, seeking to reach El Palacio to find justice by exposing the brujas to authorities. A part of the witch lore of this area is that if one sees witchcraft being practiced and keeps still, the witch will die. If he tells, he himself will die. The Spaniard had nothing to lose by exposing the brujas! However, records exist showing the hanging of witches in this frontier country, just as they were burned in Salem.

The Oldest House itself is made of puddled adobe, by the Old

Indian method in which a layer of grass-impregnated mud is poured between forms, allowed to dry, and then another layer is poured on top of the existing one. Engineering skill on the part of the Indians is demonstrated in that the walls are approximately three feet thick at the bottom, tapering down to around fifteen inches at the top.

There is now a curio shop in the Oldest House, but one room is kept more or less as it once was. It is open to the public.

GUADALUPE — The old church seen with snow

# XXI

## The Peon and the Vision

The first chapel to honor the Virgin of Guadalupe stands atop the rocky hill of Tepeyac, just outside Mexico City. It is a beautiful and impressive sight, though the immediate surroundings are not.

The visitor today — and there are thousands — may be repelled by the carnival atmosphere in the immediate vicinity of the church. Vendors hawk food and soft drinks, calling loudly over the blare of a loud speakered phonograph playing sprightly Mexican music. Fiesta-type booths dispense huaraches (Mexican sandals), gaudy plaster statuettes, cheap pot metal replicas of legs, arms, hearts, parts of the corporeal anatomy subject to diseases, serapes, tooled leather and embroidered linens. Shoe shine boys and beggars abound.

Once inside the church all of this is gone. Reverence and opulence walk side by side. Myriads of candles fail to completely pierce the dark of the high ceiling; intricate bas relief designs in gold gleam richly.

Inching up the aisles on their knees, or pulling useless legs behind them with chapped and reddened hands, peons say their beads and breathe their prayers. No one walks to the altar rail — the well-to-do are not free of pain. They, too, crawl.

Behind the altar hangs the tilma (blanket-like wrap) of Juan Diego with the imprint of the brown-skinned Virgin Mary, known as the Virgin of Guadalupe.

Juan was an Indio — a Mexican Indian — assigned to herding the sheep by the conquering Spaniard. Tepeyac hill, on this December day in 1531, wore a tilma too — one of snow, very beautiful and very cold. Juan shivered as a cutting wind knifed through his thin cotton shirt and trousers. He pulled his tilma tighter and curled his bare toes inside straw sandals. He went to mass, as he had been told to do, but this new God did not make snow any warmer than the old gods had done.

Suddenly the snow seemed to burn on the crest of the hill — blazing with rainbow radiance. Was he fainting? The bowl of corn-meal gruel that morning had been empty long before his stomach had been filled.

OLD GUADALUPE church as most tourists see it
The new church nearby lacks something

Then in the middle of the snowfire the Virgin appeared. "Go to the Bishop, my son," she told the trembling Indio softly, "and tell him to build a chapel on this spot, dedicated to me."

The way to the cathedral in Mexico City was a long one for a peon with nothing but his calloused feet to get him there, but Juan ran every step of it.

Bishop Juan de Zumarrago listened to the breathless peon and sent him back to his sheep. With all the worries he had, build a new church on the say-so of a ragged sheepherder? The man must be loco, crazed by his lonely work.

Juan trudged back to Tepeyac to gather his flock, and once again the Virgin appeared with the same message. Once again he sped to the Cathedral.

This time Zumarrago would not see him, but instructed his aide to tell the poor Indio not to come again without a sign from the Virgin herself.

Poor Juan had a footpath in the snow to follow now, but the way back to Tepeyac was no shorter. Only his breathing was that, and he feared the return. What would the Holy Mother do?

Dusk was gathering as he reached the hilltop, and the Virgin appeared for the third time. Stones were sharp under his knees as he clasped his hands and prayed. "Send me not again, Holy Mother! The

Bishop will not see me. He says I must have a sign from You to show him that I speak the truth."

The voice that answered was as gentle as summer mist as it said, "Come to this spot tomorrow and you shall have the sign." The pulsing light faded and was gone, leaving only Juan, the sheep and the biting cold.

Arriving at the tiny one room shack he called home, Juan found his uncle, who had raised him, very ill with a fever that often meant death to people in the valley of Mexico. Forgetting everything but the man who was like a father to him, Juan cared for his uncle for two days, but everything he did seemed useless. He knew that death was very close when he left to go bring a priest.

Only when he arrived close to the hill did he remember the command he had been given, the command he had failed to execute! Fearfully he panted over a path on the other side of the hill. As he passed a spring that bubbled among the rocks once again the Virgin appeared.

"Go to the hill," she commended. "The sign is there. Take it to the bishop and tell him to build the chapel and dedicate it to me."

Juan hurried to the hill top and there, blooming in the snow, was a profusion of delicately scented roses. Quickly he spread his tilma to hold them and gathered a great sheaf. The road to the cathedral

GUADALUPE DAY, December 12th, is marked with bank of roses on the altar

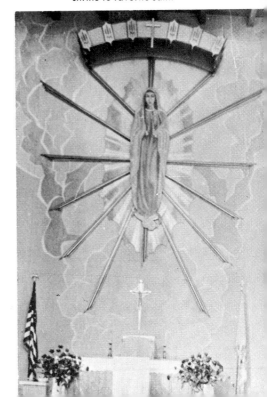

THE ALTAR in new Guadalupe church showing shrine to favorite saint

seemed shorter now. He had the sign. The day was December 12, 1531.

The good bishop at first refused to see the persistent peon, Juan, until told he had brought the sign. Skeptically he ordered the man brought to him. He would take care of this madman for once and all.

Carrying his tilma carefully Juan dropped to his knees and opened it to show Bishop Zumarago the roses. When he unfolded the tilma there was not only the unheard of roses in December, but imprinted on the tilma was the image of the Virgin exactly as She had appeared to Juan.

When Juan returned to the shabby shack of his uncle, he found that good man miraculously healed, stronger and healthier than he had been in years.

Needless to say, the chapel was built, and when the conquistadores traveled north to New Mexico, they brought with them the story of the poor Indio and reproductions of his tilma.

All over the southwest there are churches such as this one in Santa Fe dedicated to the Virgin of Guadalupe. And here and there you will see blooming in the snow the "Christmas rose."

## The Blind Man Who Could See

Buildings have character. Some are brash, noisy, painted hussies that drop their "h's" and murder the King's English. Others are very correct, cold, chromed, glassed and pinstripe-suited executives. San Miguel Chapel, on College Street (recently renamed Old Santa Fe Trail) is an ancient brown robed friar, sitting quietly in the shade of the ailanthus (tree of heaven) — telling his beads, occasionally napping; gentle, kind, patient and filled with long, long memories.

San Miguel is the oldest chapel in these United States. The voyage of the Mayflower was more than a decade in the future when orders came from far away Spain to build a new capital in this new Mexico, and the site now known as Santa Fe was chosen. The Santa Fe River ran tumultous and free, furnishing water for man and enough left over for little acequias to bathe the roots of the corn, beans and squash. There was enough flat land for milpas (fields)

**SAN MIGUEL CHURCH as seen today and as it was pictured in the 1870's**

San Miguel Church as it appeared in the 1870s. (Roberts, 1885.)

wood for fires close by, and mountains to deflect the strong winds that blow in the flatlands.

Onate and his some two hundred fifty colonists moved to the new site from San Juan de los Caballeros and began constructing El Palacio, the Palace of the Governors, probably in 1610. Across the plaza — the public square without which no Spanish village was built — they also erected a chapel, a church for the brown robed Franciscans who had come to bring a new God to the land of the Thunderbird.

Few realize that with these Spaniards were seven hundred servants, mostly Tlaxcalan Indians from Mexico. The servants lived at Barrio de Analco, across the river from the plaza, and a chapel had to be built for them. This chapel we call San Miguel.

It, too, has been dated at 1610.

Knowledgable archaeologists and learned anthropologists have studied this old chapel thoroughly. There are other old churches, but none other that has the original walls on the original site, according to Brother Lewis of San Miguel who wrote comprehensively in his "Story of San Miguel." Brother Lewis greets visitors at San Miguel today, and his hand touching a bit of woodwork, or tapping the old bell, is a gentle, understanding and knowledgable one.

San Miguel suffered extensive damage in the Revolt of 1680. Indians set fire to the vigas and the roof fell in. Surviving Spaniards had taken refuge across the river in El Palacio, watching the gradually diminishing wisps of smoke die down at Barrio de Analco. They watched

SAN MIGUEL — rear view shows massive lines

Indians bathing in the river with amole, the root of the yucca plant, to wash away their baptism.

The Spanish were able to hold on their temporary safety until the Indians diverted the water supply which went through the Plaza stronghold. Then, without horses enough for even the sick and wounded, they began the long march south, down the Rio Grande, to what is now El Paso.

It was twelve long years before the re-conquest, when Don Diego De Vargas restored Santa Fe to the Crown and the Church on September 16, 1692. Records show that by December, 1693, men were sent to the mountains to bring in new vigas to repair San Miguel, but there was too much snow and it was entirely too cold for them to fulfill their mission. By spring they were able to accomplish their project, but this repair work was either hasty or not done at all, some historians believe. Most do accept the date of 1710 for the extensive repair and rebuilding of the fallen section of walls in the then century old chapel. The three-tiered belfry tower shown in old pictures probably was not added until 1830.

Whenever the belfry was built, it seems fairly well established that it fell in 1872. There are no other accounts of any kind that record an earthquake in Santa Fe, but booklets published about San Miguel ascribe the fall of the tower to an earthquake. In all probability, Brother Lewis writes, the destruction was caused by a strong wind.

When the tower fell the oldest bell in the United States fell with it. Fortunately, it was not damaged. The history of the bell goes back

OLDEST BELL in America at San Miguel Chapel

CARVED REREDOS behind the altar, before which the blind man prayed

to Andalucia in 1356, where it was cast, and is well authenticated. This 780 pound bell is on display in the souvenir room at the chapel, and a beautiful legend is tied in with it during the time it hung in the tower.

The old, old story goes that an aged blind man came to the chapel to pray each day at noon. Feeling and tapping his way to the altar, he would drop to his knees and pray to St. Cecilia, the patron saint of music.

Though no one was near the bell rope, the ancient bell would begin to toll — it's deep throated, very beautiful tone spreading like a benediction over the area. During the time the bell tolled the blind man could see.

He described the ancient paintings, the arrow holes in the Velasquez canvas, the stations of the cross, tin candle scones, the old beam holding the choir loft — all very clearly, pointing with a shaking hand.

When the bell ceased its own prayer, the old man once again was blind. Day after day this happened, causing the devout, curious and skeptical to visit the church to see, with their own eyes, the blind man who could see so briefly, and then to watch him shuffle from the chapel, sightless again until the next day.

Legend says that when the great bell was tolled by human hands the blind man remained blind, but that the noon ringing miraculously continued until the old man died, and has not occurred in this manner since.

Thinking of this old legend and listening to the melody die away after it had been tapped by Brother Lewis today, sighted eyes somehow feel as though they might see better for having heard the ancient bell which echoes the "Saint Joseph pray for us" cast into the rim.

MIRACULOUS STAIRCASE and interior of Loretto Chapel

—Photo by Cliff Munkacsy

# XXIII

## *The Miraculous Staircase*

Santa Fe is called "The City Different" which may well be the only understatement ever made by a Chamber of Commerce. Downtown, just across a narrow one-way street from the famed La Fonda Hotel, a wayside shrine holds a life sized statue of Jesus with widespread, welcoming arms. Worn steps lead up to the statue, through a wrought iron fence and onto the grounds of Loretto Academy.

In among the huge evergreen and ancient cottonwood trees there stands a little jewel of a chapel, patterned after the Sainte-Chappele in Paris. The Academy was closed, after more than a century of service, a few years ago, but the chapel is open daily. A neat little black and white sign says "La Escalara Famosa" — the famous stair, and no trip to Santa Fe is complete without a visit to see this miraculous stair that leads to the choir loft in the chapel.

To really appreciate the stair, let us step back in time a bit. Archbishop John B. Lamy, he who contributed so much to Sante Fe, arranged in 1852 to have a small colony of the Sisters of Loretto sent to Santa Fe to found a school for young ladies.

A chapel for the school was begun 21 years later, when Archbishop Lamy hired an architect. This architect was skilled in his work, although Sister Blandina Segale, then stationed at Loretto, wrote, "He does not impress me favorably."

He evidently had trouble keeping his mind on his work, for before the chapel was completed Sister Blandina wrote in her book, "At the End of the Santa Fe Trail":

"Today our sleepy-looking — though wide awake — ancient city of Santa Fe is an agitated sea. Mr. Lamy, the Archbishop's nephew, shot and killed the new architect, and immediately surrendered to police headquarters. His bond has been fixed at $15,000. Mr. Lamy himself is making no effort to have anyone go on his bond. He prefers to be let alone and to brood over the loss of his domestic felicity. The cause of the tragedy had been repeatedly asked not to visit the Lamy residence without an invitation from him. The next step taken was that Mrs. Lamy engaged quarters at the Exchange Hotel and went there to live. Mr. Lamy warned the architect, 'Do not visit Mrs. Lamy, or I will shoot you if you do.' Today the architect was coming from Mrs. Lamy's room at the Exchange and her husband shot him dead. My impression is that His Grace knows of the tragic act — but knows nothing of what caused it."

The chapel plans could be carried out and were, only to everyone's consternation there had been no allowance made for a stairway to the choir loft. Everything was complete save only that, and what good was a choir loft with no access? Carpenters and artisans were called in. They shook their heads and left.

The black robed Sisters fingered their rosaries, and decided to make a novena to St. Joseph, patron saint of carpenters. They rose an hour early every day, entered the chapel and prayed.

On the morning of the ninth day an elderly white bearded man, leading a burro, knocked on the door of the convent. He was a carpenter, he said, and was sure he could build a stairway for them.

Delighted, Mother Superior led him to the chapel. His only tools seemed to be hammers and a saw. He asked the Sisters to bring him a couple of big tubs, and he brought, from who knows where, the lumber.

Legend differs here as to the time the carpenter worked. Some say very swiftly, others say six or eight months. Surely it was that a double helix — two complete turns of 360 degrees each — reached the choir loft with no central support of any kind, nor is there a single nail in

MIRACULOUS STAIRCASE somehow supports itself
— Photo by Cliff Munkacsy

LOOKING DOWN the miraculous staircase with a "fisheye" camera lens
— Photo by Cliff Munkacsy

the whole structure. There are thirty three steps, one for each year in the earthly life of Jesus.

Sisters told of seeing wood soaking in the tubs, but not of seeing the carpenter at work. When they came in to say their prayers, he always quietly disappeared.

There was real gratitude in the hearts of the Sisters when the stair was complete. They planned a bountiful meal in the carpenter's honor, but when they went for him he was gone.

He was never found, though they advertised for him. No lumber yard had sold him lumber. Nothing was ever paid for the building of the stair. Not only had the lumber yard men not sold the bearded man any lumber, they didn't even know what kind of wood it was that he had used. Certainly is was not any wood indigenous to this area.

But the stair stands there today, lovely to look at, a trifle dizzying to climb. Minor repairs were done on the backing in 1952. Tourists had plucked away little bits of the horsehair bound plaster at the bottom. No other repairs have been made for none have been needed.

There are those who say — and they make the sign of the cross as their lips frame the words, "Surely this miracle is the work of St. Joseph, the carpenter."

If the stair, spiraling upward, be the work of a mortal man, then it is a miracle of engineering. For believer and non-believer alike, it is indeed a miraculous stair.

LORETTO CHAPEL — Exterior view and the altar
Altar photo by Cliff Munkacsy

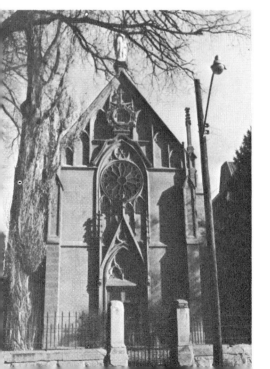

# XXIV

## Legends of the Malpais

The Spaniard, seeing the twisted, tortured dark flow of congealed lava in the shadow of Mount Taylor in Grant County, called it "mal pais" — bad country. The Indians believed this vomit of fevered earth was the blood of a great giant, killed by the war god twins. Pioneer bandits and train robbers looked upon it as an area where they couldn't be tracked, even by the most astute at reading trail signs. It remains practically unexplored at ground level, mysterious, desolate, frightening and almost impenetrable.

The lava flow, presently being considered as a national monument under twin bills introduced by Clinton P. Anderson in the Senate and Harold Runnels in the House, is one of the newest lava flows in the nation, covering an area of some 230 square miles.

Because it is so inaccessible, legends galore have sprung up — the unknown tends to produce strange and wondrous tales. Some of these yarns, as is usually the case, have at least partial historical backgrounds.

Buried treasure and lost gold mines lead in fascination for the adventurous. The malpais has both. In November of 1897, the Santa Fe train was robbed of $100,000 in gold just east of the present site of Grants. A posse was quickly organized and soon in hot pursuit through the malpais. The bandidos cached the loot to make travel easier, for the gold was heavy, and although they were caught, the loot was never recovered. In 1922 six men perpetrated another train robbery, leaving the train at the top of the Continental Divide with $30,000. That payroll money is supposedly hidden in the lava, though the bandits did get away. The story is told that they hid "the take" in the lava for safety then couldn't locate the hiding place themselves when time afforded comparative safety for retrieval. So wild and rugged are the lava beds that this would not only be possible, but easy.

In 1950, when a new highway was being cut through the lava, workers stumbled upon a small but heavy iron chest. It was badly rusted, but the contents were in good shape — $10,000 — in Confederate money. In this connection it is well to recall that the first Fort Wingate was

117

MALPAIS rocks

located approximately where the little village of San Rafael now stands and that the Confederates had many sympathizers in the Territory of New Mexico.

Brad Williams and Choral Pepper, in their book *"Lost Legends of the West"* tell the story of a Lockheed Vega that supposedly went down in the lava beds in 1936. The story goes that shortly before the national election, with F.D. Roosevelt running against Alf Landon, rumors were rife that Mexico was planning to expropriate U.S. oil company holdings south of the border. Some California oil men, believing that Landon (badly in need of campaign funds) would take a stronger stand than Roosevelt with the Mexican government, raised a "war chest" of $100,000 in cash and were having it flown by private plane to Landon. The plane, the Lockheed Vega, was last seen in the Mount Taylor vicinity. Search parties were organized but were unsuccessful. It would be very easy to lose a small plane in one of the great fissures that lace the lava beds, and perhaps it is there somewhere, waiting patiently for the lucky accident to reveal it to someone.

Grants people remember the crash that killed Mike Todd, of movie fame, but not of the Vega in 1936. That story was kept quiet at the time because of the nature of the cargo.

The "Lost Adams Diggings," number one treasure is believed by many to be in the malpais. Adams' rich find was lost when he and his companions were forced by Indians to leave their mine. It was supposed to be located so many days by mule from old Fort Wingate, but Adams himself was

118

never able to relocate his rich gold strike, though he tried for 20 years. Whether lost treasure in the lava beds will ever be recovered is, of course, moot. Certain it is that quite a collection of Indian pottery has been recovered. Jack B. Smith of Grants Chamber of Commerce will gladly show some of these finds in the fine little museum the Chamber sponsors. Skeleton finds are routine, and one skull in the collection shows that the owner met a violent death, probably by tomahawk. The hole in his head certainly looks like it!

Dave Candelaria, owner of the perpetual ice cave and Bandera Crater of the malpais, has a fine collection of pots and other artifacts of the region. Some of these he or his family have found and others have been brought in by Indians. It is believed, Candelaria says, that small bands of Indians threatened by roving bands of plains Indians took refuge in the rugged malpais and either forgot where they had hidden food and water pots or did not survive to retrieve them.

Candelaria's perpetual ice cave is as mysterious as the lava beds themselves. The cave, used by early settlers as an icehouse, has baffled scientists. There is a wall of ice 12 to 15 feet thick, and the temperature in the cave is a constant 31 degrees. Visitors now have easy access through a stairway down into the cave. Remains of old ladders still cling to the sides of the chasm showing that once it was not quite so easy as today.

A hundred yards away from the cave is the beautiful Bandera Crater, a cinder cone left from the days when this area literally spouted fire. Candelaria has hacked out pathways to the cave and cone to make it

ARTIFACTS from the lava beds

119

possible for visitors to see in comfort and safety. The family has owned this section of the malpais for several generations, and since there is no government support of any kind, there is a small fee to offset maintenance expenses.

A natural kiva, showing signs of relatively recent use, has been located on the southwest end of the lava flow. It is unique in that it contains two natural vents.

The lava beds are mysterious and guard their secrets well. Should the Park Service take over, undoubtedly a few well marked trails will replace the old cairns of stone built by Indians to mark the trails from one water hole to another and the later markers undoubtedly erected by lonely and bored sheep herders.

In the meantime, despite the antiquities act making "pot hunting" illegal, individuals continue to explore, hunting pots or treasure, Indian artifacts, or whatever may turn up.

Mount Taylor, holy mountain of the Indian world, broods as impassively over their activities as it did when Coronado marched nearby on the search for *his* lost treasure, the Seven Cities of Cibola.

BANDERA CRATER

120

EDGE OF LAVA FLOW

# Index